Angel Wings

A Story of Love,
Faith, Infertility, Surrogacy,
and Not Giving Up Hope

STEPHANIE O'HARA

PLUM BAY PUBLISHING, LLC
NEW YORK, NEW YORK
MORRISTOWN, NEW JERSEY

For permission requests, contact the publisher at the website below.
Plum Bay Publishing, LLC
www.plumbaypublishing.com

Library of Congress Control Number: 2020938447
Hardcover ISBN: 978-1-7348848-1-4
Paperback ISBN: 978-1-7348848-0-7
Ebook ISBN: 978-1-7348848-2-1

Printed in the United States of America

Cover and interior design: Barbara Aronica-Buck
Front cover photo: Art & Soul Photography by Angel Porch
Back cover author photo: Cody Giles
Editor: Brenda Aréchiga

This book is dedicated to all
infertility warriors past, present, and future.
It is my hope that the experiences I share
will bring you comfort and companionship,
elevate your perspective, and encourage you
to use your very own angel wings to
transcend your infertility, too.
This is not the end of your story.

PROLOGUE

It was late afternoon on a November day when I pulled into the vast shopping center parking lot. I put my car into park and began to sob. A few Kleenexes later, I pulled myself together and got out of my car.

"Just don't lose it when you ask the question," I told myself as I made my way toward Barnes and Noble.

The two sets of wooden doors seemed heavier than normal as I pushed them open. I inhaled the familiar smell of book paper and ground coffee, then made a quick left and walked straight up to the information desk. With her short black hair and round wire-rimmed glasses halfway down her nose, the clerk could have easily been a character straight out of a Harry Potter book.

Strangely enough, the Harry Potter section was just to the left of us toward the back of the store. I didn't know if I was going to laugh or cry when she spoke to me in an English accent.

"May I help you?"

I've never been one to speak in whispers—in fact, my husband claims it's not possible for me—but I still tried to speak softly.

"Where is your section on infertility and miscarriages?"

She looked over her glasses at me. "I'm sorry, WOT?"

I could feel the big lump in my throat as I swallowed. I was actually miscarrying, bleeding and cramping as I stood there in the store. I had just come from my OB/GYN's office. I needed information on how to cope with what I was going through. I felt so sad and incredibly alone. I felt like a failure to my husband. I also was compelled to learn about the biological aspects of what was happening to me.

"Infertility and miscarriages? Where is that section?"

"That is the oddest request! I have worked here ten years and I've never had anyone ask for those sorts of books before. We don't have anything on those subjects. I am sorry."

It was hard for me to believe that in the seemingly infinite rows of books there wouldn't be one book about miscarriage and infertility. All around me were study guides, cookbooks, countless books on dieting, and even racy titles for couples bored in the bedroom. There were books targeted at women who were pregnant and women who had lost children. How could there not be any books on miscarriage and infertility?

Tears welled up in my eyes as I walked back out into the parking lot. I wanted to punch the clerk. She couldn't have been any more cold. I wanted to scream. Something was definitely wrong with me, and I didn't know where to turn or what to do. I knew right then and there that someday, I would write my story to make this information available for women like me.

In the months and years that followed, it was a combination of my faith, personal development, and advocating for myself that helped me survive emotionally and eventually become a mother for the second and third time. It was frequently a long and lonely path, but God sent me angels who guided me in my climb.

There were times when I was angry at God. But even at my lowest point, when things were definitely not going my way, I never turned my back on God or my faith. Despite what the doctors told me, I also never completely lost hope. There were always glimmers of hope, and I chose to embrace them when they appeared.

On my journey through infertility I learned how common it is. I also learned that most women suffer in silence. The day I walked out of Barnes and Noble, I knew I would write this book. I didn't know if I would ever have children again, but I knew I would write this book to comfort, support, and offer guidance to the approximately 50 million couples worldwide who suffer from some form of infertility.

I have written my infertility memoir with heart-wrenching honesty, with the goal of restoring hope to any woman suffering from infertility. There is hope for every woman, every couple, and my wish is that they find it by reading my book.

Angel Wings

CHAPTER 1

The Golden Sun

It was the beginning of October and I was about to turn thirty. The golden sun was in my eyes as we headed west in the pasture. My weight bounced around the farm truck as my boyfriend, Dirk, made a hard-left turn, trying to avoid the cattle that were all around us. I looked up and noticed that a big, beautiful blue tent had been set up in the middle of the pasture. Just beyond it, to the west, the Oklahoma sunset melted into a rich layer of pink, blue, and purple. The gilded horizon went on for miles because the farmland was so flat.

"Now remember, there's cattle all around us," Dirk said, which was his gentlemanly way of reminding me not to step in a cow pie as I got out of the truck. His practical words were contrasted by what looked to be a romantic birthday surprise.

Surrounding the tent was a hotwire fence set up to keep out the stubborn Herefords. As I reached to pull the wire down so I could swing my leg over it, Dirk screamed.

"No, honey—! Don't touch it! I'll get it for you."

Getting electrocuted on my thirtieth birthday was not on my bucket list, so I immediately stopped. Clearly, I was a city girl. He came around to unhook the fence and chuckled. Once I was inside the tent, I looked around. I recognized an old black and blue Persian rug from Dirk's living room. On top of the rug sat a pair of well-worn captain's chairs from his dining room that he had bought at an estate sale. There were countless red roses in vases, making it look super romantic.

Over the course of our four-year relationship I had asked Dirk many times to write me a love letter. *Maybe this will be the day I will finally get one!* I thought to myself. It would be the perfect birthday gift. But instead of a letter, he had written me a beautiful poem titled "To the North Together."

Holy Cow (no pun intended), *this is happening*, was all I could think as he finished reading the poem, bent down on one knee, and took my hand.

I knew from the first time I laid eyes on Dirk that he was husband material. I was at a local pub having dinner with my girlfriends. Even though I was dating someone else, I couldn't help but notice him standing in the opposite corner from me. He was wearing a black V-neck sweater and was so handsome and refined, with strikingly beautiful blue eyes and thick, distinguished black eyebrows.

"He's totally single and quite the catch," said my roommate Linda, sipping on her beer.

As she wandered over toward him to make an introduction I realized she wasn't talking about Dirk. She was actually talking about his friend, who was standing right next to Dirk.

"No," I mouthed to her, "not him." I pointed over at Dirk. "Him!"

A look of confusion washed across Linda's face as she pointed to him and walked back over to me shaking her head. "Dirk? He's totally not your type and is in a serious relationship."

Later that night when Linda and I were walking to our car, I noticed Dirk getting into his car with his girlfriend.

"Someday, that will be me in the passenger seat . . ." I said to myself.

A few months later we crossed paths again, and he introduced himself, simply saying "I'm Dirk." He spoke in a distinct sing-song cadence. I saw immediately why Linda thought we would have nothing in common. I was an independent, spontaneous, and fun-loving girl. Everything about him was measured and disciplined. He was sophisticated and smart, yet down to earth.

Still, we both felt a connection. Our first date consisted of dinner and a few cocktails. Afterward, we went back to his house and talked late into the night. We told each other about our families and our dreams. He was an attorney who also had an MBA and was successful working in the oil and gas industry in Pennsylvania. He had returned home to Oklahoma and decided to start his own business. I was a playful, social entrepreneur and lead singer of a band. As the night went on we discovered that we were both Methodists, which seemed to intrigue him. He knew I was a singer in a band who liked to have fun, but my faith was an unexpected quality.

While Dirk had grown up in a small-town Methodist church right out of the movie *Steel Magnolias*, going to church had dropped off the radar for me when I was in high school. Coincidentally, just months before meeting Dirk I had joined a Methodist church. It also just so happened that this church had the longest aisle in the state. Like many other young women, I envisioned myself in a beautiful wedding dress with a dramatic bridal train, moving up the aisle toward the altar someday.

It was four in the morning before Dirk and I finally stopped talking that first night. He was different from the other guys I had dated. I was at a place in my life where a man who could be my rock and who also loved a good dirty joke was very attractive to me.

From the very beginning we brought out the best in one another. Dirk would sometimes frustrate me—raising the bar and pushing me to climb higher. But he truly made me want to be a better person who overcame obstacles and achieved goals. I, in turn, helped Dirk, who was very focused, to become a more affectionate boyfriend and learn to slow down to stop and smell the roses. We were the perfect balance.

Back to the proposal. As we sat in the tent in the middle of the cow pasture, Dirk began explaining the symbolism of all that surrounded us. Everything in the tent meant something. The ugly rug that he loved (and I hated) represented compromise. The vintage chairs symbolized us growing old together, side by side. The Waterford crystal vase was part of his Irish heritage, and the red roses stood for love.

Dirk's thumb nervously rubbing the top of my hand focused me back in. He was still on bended knee.

"Will you grow old with me and have my five children?"

I looked into his eyes. My answer was obviously yes! I squealed. Once I had responded, he pulled out my engagement ring. In the last year, I had continually dropped hints about my ring size, the kind of setting I liked, the diamond cut . . . but Dirk never seemed interested in the conversation and would always change the topic. As he slipped the ring on my finger, I sat there in awe. I could feel it was the wrong size and noticed that it didn't have any kind of stone at all. In true Dirk fashion, this totally could have been picked up at an estate sale.

"Do you like your ring?"

"Yes!" I paused and looked at him. "Honey, I am so excited to become your wife that I would say yes to a piece of tin foil wrapped around my finger."

The truth was I did love my ring. Even though it wasn't what I had ever imagined it would be, the fact that Dirk had picked it out with me in mind made me love it. We popped a bottle of champagne and toasted one another.

"You're sure you like your ring?" Dirk asked me again.

"Yes."

Then, from his pocket he pulled out a crushed velvet ring box. "Well, that's too bad, because this is your real ring." He opened up the box and there it was—my ring—exactly as I had described it to him all of those months. I gushed as he slipped it on my finger and smiled, knowing he had been listening to me all along. Dirk's parents, Forrest and Loretta, drove up in a farm truck and joined us for a toast.

As I sipped on my champagne and watched the sunset from my captain's chair in the pasture, I admired my ring and excitedly thought about my future with Dirk and our five children. My mind went into overdrive wondering if my petite frame could handle five pregnancies. Maybe Dirk and I would settle on three. It was time to get busy—I had a wedding to plan!

CHAPTER 2

Where Do We Go Now?

Our wedding was beautiful. Just as I had envisioned, our ceremony was held in the church with the longest aisle in town. I had spent many Sundays dreaming how my dress and train would flow down that long, beautiful aisle. The church had tall, gorgeous stained-glass windows throughout. Hundreds of candles were lit. For dramatic flair, after the last guest had been seated, the large wooden sanctuary doors closed and a bagpiper began to play, making his way up the aisle.

When the bagpiper arrived at the front of the church, the pipe organ joined in. This was the cue for me to step into the church on my father's arm, and finally become Mrs. O'Hara.

"You okay, Dad?"

My father, whom we affectionately refer to as Chucky C., nodded as a tear rolled down his cheek. He was so emotional—giving away his eldest daughter. As he grabbed his cane, I began to wonder if his tear wasn't actually from pain. You see, the day before, he had taken some wedding guests from out-of-town to lunch. On the way out the door in a style only my dad can possess, he fell straight back into a big flower pot. He literally landed sitting down inside the pot, throwing his back out in the process. So now, on my wedding day, he could hardly walk and winced with each step down that long aisle. I tried not to giggle as I said a prayer that we could make it to the altar.

I have no doubt that my dad probably had wondered if I would ever get married. I didn't have a great track record in the dating department.

In fact, he had told many of my previous boyfriends that they would be lucky to last ninety days.

As I walked up the aisle I tried to take in as many faces as I could. Our wedding was large; Dirk and I had invited friends from childhood, high school, and college. We have both been fortunate enough to have such wonderful people around us, and wanted to make sure we shared our special moments with them all. I tried to savor those few minutes walking up the aisle—knowing that *never* in my life was I going to have all of those people in a room together again. When I finally arrived at the altar, I thought Dirk had never looked so handsome.

"Who gives this woman to be married to this man?"

"Her mother and I do," my dad said as he winced in pain, kissed me, and hobbled to sit next to my mom.

Our reception was as crazy as our ceremony was special! Still in my wedding dress, I paid tribute to the love of music that runs in my family's veins by singing four songs. My bandmates joined me on stage and we played songs by Meatloaf and The Cranberries. I will never forget the hilarious moment when my Aunt Nancy and Cousin Joe sang the chorus from Guns & Roses' "Sweet Child of Mine." It was a crowd favorite.

After the reception we moved the party over to our hotel suite, where we celebrated with fifty or so of our closest friends. By five in the morning, I was exhausted and decided it was time to go to bed. Dirk and his friends were still going strong. We had talked earlier in the night and agreed that we would spend our wedding night with friends. We had our whole honeymoon to be romantic. Valerie, one of my bridesmaids, helped me out of my wedding dress. I climbed into the bridal bed, which was covered in rose petals and Hershey's Kisses, thanks to my sweet sister. I woke up later in the morning in my white lace underwear and briefly glanced at myself in the mirror as I made my way to the bathroom. My heart started beating fast. I stopped and backed up. My entire backside was covered in some sort of brown, thick paste. After briefly thinking that I had pooped myself on my wedding night, I remembered.

"Hershey's Kisses!" I said to myself. I can always count on my sister for some laughter.

CHAPTER 3

No Offense to Blondes

The entire time Dirk and I were dating, my hair was platinum. Then one day, he finally confessed that he wasn't normally attracted to blondes. Even though he met and fell in love with me while I had bleached hair, he still liked to make blonde jokes and I in turn liked to give him a hard time about his hang-up with blondes.

I had been dyeing my hair for so long, I had no idea what my natural hair color was anymore. I had given my hairstylist free reign on my hair and she never disappointed! Since I was the lead singer of a rock band, I thought it was important to have edgy, eclectic, and cool hair. My girl-friends Valerie, Tracey, Linda, Missy, and I all went to her and had similar cuts. Every six weeks, we spent hours in her chair having her create new looks for us. For several years, I had a short wedge cut. Then there was the graduated bob. I also had a Jenna Elfman–inspired "Dharma-Do." There were so many different hairstyles, but I was consistently blonde in some form or fashion: platinum, brassy, streaked—you name it, I had it!

After we were engaged, Dirk convinced me to go with my natural hair color, whatever that would be. Turns out, it was chestnut brown; who knew! In the process, I was hundreds of dollars richer and I had gained at least three hours every six weeks.

Our first year of marriage was spent having fun, traveling, and build-ing a strong foundation for our lives together. Even though we had agreed on a large family, we felt it was important to spend this time together, just the two of us. We were both very busy building our careers and I had gone back to finish my degree.

You see, I had floundered in college the first time around. Lord knows I made a lot of poor choices back then. For two years I dated someone who was violent and abusive. I fell into a deep, dark depression; I felt completely hopeless and thought there was no way out. Eventually, I stopped going to class and would sleep way past noon every day. Then one night—it happened. He went on a rage, beat me, and locked me in a closet. He then began punching holes in the walls of my apartment. A neighbor heard this happening and called campus police. My parents were called and immediately came to my side. I dropped out of college, left my sorority, and moved home. It was quite a humbling experience.

Remember I mentioned that Dirk was always raising the bar and pushing me higher? This was one of those times. After meeting Dirk, I was inspired to try college again. Once I succeeded in getting my bachelor's degree, I had a hunger to continue to learn and achieve. I wanted to prove that I could do anything I put my mind to. It's something that drives me to this day, probably to a fault at times.

It was after our second wedding anniversary that we decided it was time to start our family. After three months of negative pregnancy tests, I started tracking my ovulation, which was extremely stressful and very unromantic. I began implementing my own creative ways to increase my odds of becoming pregnant such as doing naked handstands or elevating my hips in bed for ten minutes after sex. Dirk would just shake his head and laugh when he found me inverted, feet up on the wall behind me.

Up until now, the timeline of my life had happened perfectly, pretty much the way I had planned. I assumed because I was still young and healthy that I would get pregnant right away. Yet for the better part of the year, my period arrived right on schedule. Every month, I sat on the toilet, crying. My awareness was heightened, so every time I turned on the TV,

I would see a commercial with a darling baby staring at me. I would go to the grocery store and run into someone who had a baby bump. Everywhere I went, everything reminded me that I was not pregnant, but the rest of the world was. I had flashes of Dirk on bended knee, proposing marriage and asking me to have his five children. One day in the tampon aisle at Target I wanted to lie down on the cold tile and do the "ugly cry," as I call it. I begged God to give us a baby.

After the sixth month, I started to feel like a failure. My body wasn't doing what it was supposed to do; it was failing me. The pressure was mounting, and it felt as though Dirk was growing impatient with me.

I couldn't help but feel there was something wrong with me. Finally, I decided to take a break from worrying about it. I had a lot on my plate and needed to focus on those things.

The winter after our third wedding anniversary we took a trip to Costa Rica. We had heard the country was beautiful, unspoiled and uncommercialized. The Junior League charity ball was scheduled for two months after our return from Costa Rica and I was one of the organizers. My graduation from the Master's program was just two weeks after that. Between finishing my thesis, studying for finals, organizing auction items, and finalizing details of the charity ball, I had no time to think about getting pregnant.

The next couple of months flew by and before I knew it, it was the day of my graduation. My whole family and Dirk's family attended the ceremony, and afterward we all gathered together at our house for a big backyard party that I had been looking forward to.

At the party, where I could finally relax, my mom, who can out-talk anybody about anything, walked straight over to me where I was sipping a glass of champagne.

"Your boobs are enormous!"

My mom, a retired schoolteacher, looked like a beautiful, fair-skinned Shirley MacLaine. We teased each other quite a bit—it was our love language. I figured this was her way of telling me that what I was wearing was too revealing. It was too late for me to change my clothes so I smiled, said "Thanks, Mom!" and kept dancing. She wandered away, undoubtedly to chat with someone else.

A couple of days later at the Junior League Monday night meeting, a tiredness came over me. I couldn't keep my eyes open. As the meeting continued, the only voice I could focus on was my own in my head.

"Well, it's finally hit me. All of the craziness from the last few months has caught up to me in the form of exhaustion."

We usually went to dinner after the meeting, but I was genuinely concerned I would fall asleep in my Margherita pizza. I made my excuses and walked to my car, which was parked across the street from Walgreen's.

The red neon lights of the drugstore called to me.

"Could I? There's no way."

I had taken several pregnancy tests the last year, only to be disappointed. Against my better judgment I slipped into the brightly lit drugstore, found the family planning aisle, and bought a pregnancy test. This time it was a digital one that promised the fastest, most accurate reading. My mind raced as I drove the five miles to my house. I caught every red light. It seemed like an eternity before I finally pulled into my driveway.

When I walked into the house, I went straight to the bathroom and took the test. As I flushed, I really wasn't expecting it to be positive. I set the stick up on the counter and washed my hands. When I finished, I looked over and there it was—a faded, faded blue. I was pregnant! Wait, what?

I did a double take. I was shocked. Pregnant!

Dirk was out of town on business, so I went to bed that night and enjoyed my little secret—I had our baby inside me. I was relieved and scared at the same time. I also knew that it was miraculous and divine. I took a big, deep breath, exhaled, and went to sleep.

The next day I went to the Hallmark store and bought a figurine of a woman holding a baby. At the base of the figurine was the word *Mother*. Dirk would be back that night, so I wrapped up the box and handed it to him when he got home.

"I think I found my new profession, now that my school career is finally over." I giggled.

Dirk opened the gift, looked at me, and turned the figurine in his hands as if it were a puzzle.

"I don't get it."

"Read the word at the bottom, Honey."

I watched his eyes lower and process the word: *Mother*. He was in complete shock, just as I had been.

"I'm pregnant! You're going to be a daddy."

He was completely shocked.

After what seemed like about twenty minutes of silence, I had to say something.

"Are you excited?"

"Yes. Yes, I am." And then he smiled and kissed me.

Within a week of finding out I was pregnant, I went shopping for maternity clothes. I just couldn't help myself! A wave of emotion washed over Dirk as I walked toward him to kiss him good-bye and head to an early morning meeting. He pulled me toward him and gave my belly a very tender kiss.

"This is getting exciting," Dirk said. His cute bed head and sleepy eyes only added charm to the moment.

This was more of the reaction I had been anticipating on the night

I broke the news to Dirk. I understood that he was a man who needed to see proof, and here it was. I spent my days thinking and dreaming of our baby. It was the most precious and important time. I already felt connected to the baby by the most incredible maternal bond.

I spent most of my first trimester exhausted and napping through *30 Minute Meals with Rachael Ray* in the evenings after work. Of course, there was no point in even trying to watch Rachael Ray when you consider the fact that I could no longer go into a grocery store without gagging. The smell of the rotisserie chickens, which I usually bought once a week, now made me feel like I was going to vomit right there under the fluorescent lights.

Chocolate, however, was my new best friend. Every morning I drove to the donut shop near our house and ordered a chocolate milk in a mini carton and a chocolate-covered donut. After a few months, the cashier had it ready for me every morning by the time I got out of my car and waddled inside. In the afternoon, after I woke up from my Rachael Ray nap, I drove to Braum's, our local ice cream and burger joint, and ordered a medium-size chocolate milkshake at the drive-through. I gained over fifty pounds in my pregnancy, which was almost half of my pre-pregnancy weight.

Growing up, when I gained a couple of pounds it always showed in my stomach. Even though I had a petite frame, I always had a little bulge, which caused me to have a bit of a complex. While I was pregnant, I just enjoyed eating my chocolate and rocked my pregnant belly.

Early in the second trimester we found out we were having a boy. As I lay there on the vinyl-upholstered table in the OB's office with the technician moving the ultrasound paddle around my belly, Dirk's eyes brightened and he gave an enthusiastic "Wahoo!" and kissed me. I was so excited—I always wanted a boy. Truthfully, I was also relieved to give Dirk his namesake, a son to carry on the farm and the family name.

As soon as we left the doctor's office, I called my younger sister, Melanie, to share the news. She was taller than I, but we shared the same skinny bird legs. She had our dad's big beautiful blue eyes and was full of personality.

A silence fell over the phone conversation as soon as the word *boy* left my lips. It lasted about twenty seconds. She was absolutely *sure* I was having a girl.

"Con . . . grat . . . u . . . la . . . tions . . . " she had said to us on speakerphone in the car. There was complete silence. My sister was stunned.

"Mel—are you excited for us?" I asked.

"Yes! But Steph, we don't know what to do with a boy."

She wasn't wrong. There were just girls in our family. We had spent our childhoods playing with dolls. As teens we did each other's hair and makeup, and my sister was still all about the glitz and glam.

Even though my sister was correct in her observation that we didn't know what to do with a boy, knowing the gender deepened my bond with my little baby even more. The biggest milestone came unexpectedly on our "BabyMoon" to Los Angeles, where I splurged on a facial at the hotel spa. I was lying flat on my back and I felt an air bubble in my stomach. Then there was another one about three minutes later. It was my baby, whom I had begun calling "Baby O," saying hello to me.

At thirty-seven weeks, right after the new year, we had an examination performed by my OB, Dr. Allison, whom I had been going to for several years. She and her staff were warm, with a friendly bedside manner. I felt fortunate to have her guiding me through my pregnancy and delivering my baby. As her cold hands moved around my abdomen, a look of surprise washed over her face.

"Oh." She paused as she felt around. "Oh, my. This baby's head is very large. How far along are we?"

She looked at my chart. "We need to schedule an induction before this baby gets any bigger."

I was still three weeks from my due date, but I certainly heeded the warning. Dirk and I had been going to child-birthing classes and we had seen enough video footage to know that it was excruciating in even the best of circumstances. I didn't want to put my health or the baby's at risk by waiting to go into labor naturally.

The doctor pulled out her calendar and Dirk and I went over it with her. January 8th was Elvis Presley's birthday. This historical fact seemed to convince Dirk.

"Let's have him share a birthday with the King."

January 8th it was.

The night before the surgery was very strange and surreal. Dirk and I kept thinking we should do something special on our last night as just the two of us, like go to dinner or a movie, but in the end we didn't do anything. The finishing touches had been put on the baby's room. The car seat had been installed and our overnight bags were packed. We were nervous and excited. I was worried that I wouldn't be able to fall asleep that night, but luckily I did. Little did I know that I wouldn't get that kind of sleep for quite some time.

Early the next morning we drove to the hospital. It was still dark outside and the winter chill hit us as we walked to the car. We held hands in the car knowing we were driving to go have our baby, who we already loved so much.

After we checked into the hospital, I was taken to my private room on the labor and delivery floor. Within a few minutes, I put on the lightly patterned hospital gown and climbed into the bed. My nurse came in, introduced herself and explained she was going to start an IV. The needle burned as she pierced my skin with it. Once it was in she taped it down and hung up the bag full of Pitocin, the drug used to induce labor.

Within an hour, Dr. Allison came in and broke my water. They placed a fetal monitor on my baby and turned on the sound so that we could hear his heartbeat. A blood pressure cuff that would take automatic readings every fifteen minutes was placed on my arm.

It was very calm and quiet in the room. I settled into the bed and Dirk sat in the vinyl recliner at my side. He read the newspaper and answered a few phone calls from family members. A couple of hours later, there was a commotion in the hallway. I knew instinctively it was my family, which Dirk always likened to a tsunami. They rolled in as usual— my dad talking loudly on his cell phone and my mother arguing with him, telling him to get off of the damn phone. They had four briefcases, bags, and even a suitcase with them.

My sister lost it as soon as she walked into the room and saw me in my hospital gown with tubes and wires connected to me. She became emotional very easily, which I loved her for. I laughed and calmed her down. As overwhelming as they can be, it was comforting to have my family at my side, since my job for the afternoon was just to sit in the bed and be patient.

Around noon my doctor came in to examine me.

"You still haven't progressed. We'll wait a few more hours."

I was disappointed to hear that my cervix wasn't dilating. The doctor was giving me Pitocin to cause contractions and trigger labor, but Baby O was not responding. I wandered (okay, waddled) the halls trying to induce labor. I wanted him to come out if only so I could have a drink of water.

Four hours later my family and I had talked ourselves to death. My throat and my tongue were like sandpaper. My thirst was unbearable. Getting a drink of water was the only thing I could think about. At four in the afternoon, my doctor strolled in and called it. I was still only dilated to one. Baby O would be delivered by Caesarean section.

Before I knew it, they were wheeling me down to the surgery room, where a male nurse anesthetist was waiting for me. The floors were bright and the lights buzzed overhead. The anesthesiologist was in blue scrubs and a blue cap. He was very comforting to me and explained what he was doing each step of the way. I felt the stinging of the thick epidural needle as it went into my back. I looked up at him, blinded by the bright lights above his head. I was so parched, I could barely speak.

"I'm going to die of thirst."

The anonymous surgical nurse strapped my arms down on either side of me and set up a curtain at my breasts so I couldn't see the lower part of my body. Then I turned to Dirk, who was standing at my shoulder wearing a paper hair net, and gave him strict orders. "You stay at my side. I don't want you seeing my guts." Dirk laughed.

After a minute I grew dazed and woozy the way you do after a couple of cocktails. I didn't feel any pain, but there was a distinct feeling of pressure and tugging on my abdomen. I had no sense of time but after what seemed like half an hour, the doctor gasped excitedly.

"Dirk, you've got to come over here and see this."

"Doc, she told me I can't peek over the curtain."

The doctor laughed and insisted, at which point Dirk looked down at me.

"Can I?"

I had no idea what could be going on down there. Clearly nothing was wrong if the doctor sounded so joyful and calm. I nodded at Dirk and he took a few steps down toward the doctor. I wanted so badly to know what he was seeing.

"Honey, is there anything you need to tell me? Does the milkman have blond hair?" The operating room erupted in laughter.

Although it was super funny, I was dying to see my baby. Dirk had the biggest smile on his face when they brought the baby over to me. We had already been together for nine months and here he was, our little miracle. We locked eyes, and a little door in my heart that I didn't even know existed opened up. I stared into our baby's eyes and kissed him full on the lips. Tears streamed down my face.

"Happy birthday, little one! It's so nice to finally meet you! I love you so much."

I knew then that God had a sense of humor. My baby, who was just so perfectly beautiful, had a full head of platinum blond hair the exact shade mine had been for so many years.

CHAPTER 4

The Anomaly

After being stapled and sewn, I was wheeled back into my empty hospital room while our baby boy was being cleaned up. "I'm a mom," I thought to myself incredulously. It had been a long day, so I was enjoying the peace and quiet of being alone for just a moment. I was exhausted and incredibly parched, as if I had been out in the hot desert for days without anything to drink, but I was so thankful my baby was healthy. I felt pure bliss. Even though I had just met our little boy, I loved him so much. For the first time, I was experiencing unconditional love.

It wasn't long before I heard my family out in the hallway. Despite hospital rules, my dad was on his phone with one of our relatives and my mom was using her schoolteacher voice to my father—for being on the phone. He wasted no time making himself right at home in the recliner next to my bed. Melanie was still on a roller coaster of emotions and came into the room crying, carrying an armful of gifts for her new nephew. Dirk's brother and my in-laws floated in quietly behind my family along with my friends Libbi, Stacy, and Melissa, who had spent all day waiting in the lobby.

It was standing room only when Dirk, my doctor, and one of the delivery nurses proudly rolled in with our new baby in a clear plastic bassinet. He was covered with a lightweight cotton blanket and was wearing a blue cap on his head that was crocheted by a hospital volunteer. In the delivery room, Dirk had shared with the doctor a prank that we had schemed up. It had made her laugh out loud and exclaim, "Oh, I have to stay for this!"

From the moment we found out we were having a boy, Dirk and I knew what we were going to call him. The name was Dirk's idea, but I loved it too since it was an old family name full of history and tradition. We kept the name to ourselves, waiting to reveal it when our son was born. Until then we continued calling him "Baby O."

Everybody crowded around the bassinet gasping at the new addition to our family. Dirk's facial expression remained completely serious as he pulled the blanket off the baby.

"Everyone, we would like for you to meet Presley . . . Hereford . . . O'Hara."

It was no surprise that everyone's jaw hit the floor. My mom and sister looked as if they had just taken a big gulp of sour milk. My father-in-law just shook his head in disgust. Today was in fact the birthday of Elvis Presley, and Herefords were the cows my father-in-law raised on his farm. Needless to say, the idea of his grandchild sharing the name of the King of rock 'n' roll and the cattle he raised came as a shock. I was so sleepy from the anesthesia I could hardly keep my eyes open. Both of our families fired away with the questions. My father, who had submitted his own list of suggested names, did a double take.

"I'm sorry. What? What's his name?"

Dirk removed our little boy's cap from his head. "Here's the best part. Check out his hair!" Everybody gushed over his spikey, inch-long platinum blond hair. Our moms both cooed over him. The nurse who had been delivering babies for many years weighed in with her professional opinion.

"In my twenty years as a labor and delivery nurse, he is only the second baby I've seen that was born with a full head of platinum blonde hair. I don't know if you realize how special and rare this is, but he is quite an anomaly."

After about ten minutes Dirk decided it was time to let everyone off the hook. "Hey guys, his name isn't really Presley Hereford." My doctor, who was in on the joke, couldn't help but laugh. Dirk left it to me to announce his real name.

"His name is Aidan Phillips."

As soon as I said our baby's real name, my father-in-law's eyes welled up with tears. Everyone else looked visibly relieved, and they all exhaled. Dirk and I loved the name for its definition; ardent and fiery, but we also knew the special significance of the name in the O'Hara family. Three generations prior, in the 1880s, Dirk's great-grandmother Mary Sinnott had left her home in Enniscorthy, Ireland, making the daunting trip across the Atlantic on her own when she was only fourteen years old.

After meeting her Irish husband in the northeastern part of the United States, Mary and her husband traveled down south to line up for a parcel of land in the Oklahoma Land Run of 1889. Mary would end up giving birth to nine boys; the first two sons were twins, whom she named Barnard and Aidan. Aidan was named after the Victorian cathedral church dedicated to St. Aidan that she had attended at home in Enniscorthy. The story was very similar to the movie *Far and Away* with Nicole Kidman and Tom Cruise.

We loved giving our first-born son a name that could be traced back to his roots in Ireland.

Phillips was the maiden name of both my paternal grandmother and Dirk's maternal grandmother. I glanced over at my father, who was shaking his head and looking confused.

"What is his first name? Can you say it again? How do you spell that?"

I laughed so hard it hurt.

Even though we spelled it for him, my father still couldn't pronounce it after four tries. I knew then it was time to get the family out of the room.

My family left after an hour and went to a Mexican restaurant across the street. I talked Dirk into joining them so he could have his first real meal of the day. All day long I had thought that as soon as it was over, I'd get to have a giant hamburger for dinner. I realized I was sorely mistaken when a nurse came in and set down a little packet of saltine crackers on my tray. She also came in bearing two bottles of Gatorade and a can of Sprite. I drank all of them in just in an hour's time.

The fatigue was really starting to set in, but I couldn't stop staring at Aidan with a complete sense of wonder. He had been inside me for nine months and now that he was here, I couldn't stop staring at him! Even though he was just hours old I knew he was an old soul. I could see my mother in him; they shared the distinct almond-shaped eyes that came from the Choctaw Indian in her family.

As we sat in our room, it was quiet time for me, Aidan, and God. Bringing another soul into the world was already a more awe-inspiring experience than I had the words to describe. I absolutely didn't take it for granted that we had both come through the pregnancy and the delivery safely. Even though he hadn't expressed it in the same way, I could tell Dirk was having similar feelings. In the first hour after our baby was born, while we were still in the operating room, he gave me a very tender kiss.

"Steph, if this is the only child you're able to have, it's okay."

I appreciated his words, but the sentiment was uncharacteristic of Dirk. He had never been shy about wanting to have a big Irish family. Asking me to have his five children had been part of his marriage proposal. For him to express anything else told me his heart was as full as mine.

Dirk was very tired, happy, and a little buzzed from a couple of beers when he came back from dinner. The owner of the restaurant had brought out two rounds of celebratory cerveza for the whole family. Having spent all day in a hospital, it wasn't surprising that Dirk had come down with a terrible cold. I watched him take Aidan in his arms, being careful to divert his breath out the left side of his mouth and away from our newborn son.

I laughed at the *pfoooo* sound he made every time he exhaled. It was hilarious! We were both so giddy as we stared at Aidan. I thought back to that night more than eight years ago when I laid eyes on Dirk for the very first time. Now our love had produced a miracle, our special little boy, who I knew was destined for wonderful things.

CHAPTER 5

Motherhood Adjustment

In the last few hours of our hospital stay, the chaos in our room made me think we should extend our time there. I had checked into the hospital with a big binder full of crucial newborn information, and now, after back-to-back-to-back consultations with the pediatrician, lactation specialist, and post-op team, the rings on my binder refused to close.

"Can I please stay another day?"

My favorite nurse was not sympathetic. "No. Get out," she said half-jokingly.

Although I was excited to get home, I knew it was going to be tough. I was going to have to take care of Aidan and I was figuring out that somebody was going to have to take care of me.

On the day of Aidan's birth, I didn't have any sense of worry until the meds wore off late that night. It was incredibly painful. I had a huge incision across my abdomen that had been closed with giant staples. My stomach was swollen from the incision in my uterus and from having my abdominal muscles moved aside. I could tell from the pressure and tightness that my organs had been moved around, and now they felt like they were floating in outer space.

Two nurses came in that night to help me get out of bed and walk around the room. I was wearing compression devices on my legs that started at my ankles and went up to my thighs. They tightened and released, making my legs and feet soooooooo uncomfortable.

It was the next day, when Dirk and a nurse helped me up out of bed and into the bathroom, that it finally hit me: I had undergone major surgery. I mean, major. I couldn't bend over because of my incision. There was blood and iodine all over the bottom half of my body and I couldn't even wash myself without help. Between having my boobs groped earlier by an unfamiliar La Leche lactation specialist and now having a strange woman help me bathe in front of my hubby, I didn't know how much more of a humbling experience it could be.

"Honey, could I have some privacy?"

Dirk stepped out of the bathroom without any protest. I recognized my body was completely traumatized. My thoughts may have been shallow, but I felt like a big, fat cow and I didn't want Dirk to see me this way.

I was in agony. One of the nurses gave me a pain pill. I didn't think to ask what it was, but it made me see triple. It was so strong that I actually had to close my eyes just to be able to focus.

It hadn't taken long for the responsibility of being a new mommy to sink in. Even though my mom would be staying with me for a couple of weeks and Dirk would be working from home the first week, eventually they would go back to their normal routines. With everything I had to manage, I was scared to be by myself.

"This is it. We're on our own," I thought as we checked out of the hospital. I rode in the backseat of our SUV next to Aidan in his car seat. He slept for the duration of the five-mile drive to our house. When we got home, my mother pulled in behind us. We stopped to take a photo of me, Dirk, and Aidan at our front door.

It felt so good to be back home. Once inside, we took him straight into his nursery, put him in his bassinet, and just stared at our beautiful, sweet little boy.

As it is done in the south, humanity surrounds you when you have a baby. Our friends had organized a meal train for us so we wouldn't have to worry about cooking dinner for almost three months. It was glorious. Every other night between five and six o'clock, dinner was delivered by our friends. Usually whoever had brought dinner stayed for about an hour and held Aidan so that we could eat.

Even with all the support we had, there were challenges that were outside of our control. Our first night at home with Aidan was so hard. He cried all night. It didn't matter how long or how many times I nursed him, he just wailed. The very next morning we were exhausted and concerned. Dirk and I took him straight back to the hospital, where I found myself talking to the same La Leche lactation specialist. Our initial meeting had been within the first hour after Aidan's birth. She wasn't any more comforting this time around. "Let me watch you," she said as she manhandled my boob.

I unbuttoned my blouse, unclasped my nursing bra, and nestled Aidan into the crook of my arm. His little mouth latched onto my nipple. I felt like some lab animal under observation. "Don't give up, your milk just hasn't come in yet," she said as I tucked my giant cantaloupe of a breast back into my bra.

We returned home without any answers. Aidan continued to cry. I was frantic and felt like my body was failing. Aidan was still crying the next morning, so we returned to the hospital for our third consultation with the La Leche specialist. She was as aggressive as ever and still didn't have any answers.

"Doesn't he need to eat?" I knew in that moment that I would have to be my own champion, and Aidan's. The question I was about to ask was going to go over like a lead balloon, but I asked anyway.

"I'm going to get some baby formula on my way home, so can you recommend one I should buy?" As I had expected, she offered no recommendation.

When my milk came in I felt an excruciating sensation of pins and needles in my breasts.

"Shit, shit, shit!" I would scream.

I used my breast pump to conduct my own experiment and learned I was only producing an ounce of milk at a time. An ounce! Aidan needed two to three times that, according to the big binder. All this time I had been starving him, so it was no surprise that he had lost over a pound in his first week. I felt terrible.

"I've been starving him and I didn't even know it!" I cried to Dirk.

All of my friends were champs at this breastfeeding thing. I felt like a complete failure.

Once I had solved the riddle, I would breastfeed Aidan for thirty minutes and then bottle feed him for another thirty minutes. I repeated this every three hours, and finally his crying stopped.

Even though I was still recovering from my C-section, I loved taking care of Aidan. It was such important bonding time with him. I was also enjoying having all this special time with my own mom. I was home-bound and still couldn't lift anything or bend over. It was only in the last day or so that I had been able to shower on my own. Aside from my mom just being incredibly helpful, it was really neat to bond with her. She was feeling very nostalgic, and we reminisced about her pregnancies and her early days with me. Being a mom now gave me a whole new appreciation for her and for motherhood.

I felt like Super Mom when I got up with Aidan in the middle of the night. It was just the two of us in his nursery. I whispered sweet nothings into his ear as I fed him, burped him, and changed his diapers. Sometimes we had quiet time, and other times we watched infomercials for juicers, skincare, and stain removers.

As the time approached for my mom to go back home, I grew very emotional. Here I was, thirty-four years old, and I was having separation anxiety about my mom leaving. "I'm responsible for this human being," I thought to myself. "I'm not ready." I wanted my mom.

In addition to taking care of a newborn baby and managing our home, I was also still running my business. Although it was a well-oiled machine and I had assigned someone to manage it while I was on maternity leave, the pressure was still there. Soon it would be time to submit a bid to renew my contract with the U.S. government. For the past four years, I had provided transportation for government personnel for the Federal Aviation Administration. Although it was lucrative, the thought of writing this bid between feeding the baby, doing laundry, washing bottles, recovering from surgery, and sleeping overwhelmed me. My mother-in-law was stopping by now and again to help, but I was still struggling.

It had been a month since I had given birth, but my hormones were still dumping. I could feel myself becoming more emotional. I spent one afternoon lying on the couch with Dirk—just crying uncontrollably in his arms. Dark thoughts started popping into my head. I found myself worrying and obsessing about ways in which Aidan could get hurt. Plastic packaging from a Bed Bath and Beyond comforter that was in our closet, which until recently had seemed innocuous, could kill him. Sitting in front of the warm fireplace wasn't an option because Aidan could die in there. The patio located off of a room on the second story was now dangerous and something from which Aidan could fall to his death.

I knew these weren't normal thoughts, but I didn't want to talk to anyone about them. I was embarrassed, quite frankly. I had all these successful women around me and didn't want to be judged as being incompetent.

Before too long I felt like I was carrying around a boulder in a backpack and was collapsing under the weight. "I can't believe I agreed to do this four more times," I said to myself, thinking about the five children I had committed to when Dirk proposed. I knew then it was time to talk to him. I was so embarrassed about my feelings and terrified he would deem me untrustworthy with Aidan. Even though he couldn't relate to my feelings, he was very supportive and encouraged me to call my doctor.

I couldn't believe that after mustering up the courage to talk to Dirk and now call my doctor, the response was so routine. They immediately offered to call in a prescription for an antidepressant. Although I was open to their remedy, I also knew I wanted to address the core issue and not just put a Band-Aid on my problem. I pressed them for the name of a good counselor.

I tried to downplay how I was feeling when I made my first call to the counselor. I had so much shame and thought nobody could possibly have problems like I did. Aidan was already three months old, and now I was the one who couldn't stop crying.

Our niece Beth, who was a college student, came over to watch Aidan while I went to my first counseling appointment. The office was only five miles away and close enough to Dirk's office that I could stop in to see him.

The counselor was in a simple one-room office. She had short blonde hair and a friendly demeanor that made me comfortable right away. I took a seat on the couch across from the chair where she was sitting and shared how I was feeling. I couldn't believe how freeing it felt to speak the truth. She smiled at me compassionately before she spoke.

"You're just adjusting to motherhood. It's truly the hardest job in the world."

I sobbed. I sat there on the couch clutching the wet crumbled sheets of Kleenex. I was so relieved she understood. There was a name for what I was going through. I had post-partum depression—and I wasn't alone. Twenty percent of women who give birth each year were affected by it. "You don't have to love every second of motherhood," she continued.

"Sometimes it stinks and can be incredibly hard." A friend had told me the same thing. I felt relief that I wasn't the only one.

My homework from our first session was to take every day "one minute at a time." It was easier said than done. The waves of emotion would randomly wash over me and I would cry uncontrollably. I heeded her advice and took it hour by hour.

Every week I looked forward to going to see her. She had an independent view and understood my feelings. I also figured out pretty quickly that stopping by Dirk's office afterward so we could process things together was not productive. This was not a problem he could solve.

After each session, it took me two days to process what I discussed with the counselor. After a couple of weeks, I could feel the dark clouds lifting. We focused on developing coping mechanisms like writing in a journal and exercising. Beth would come over a couple of times a week so I could go to Pilates, the office, counseling sessions, and the grocery store. One evening a week, Dirk and I would have date night. I looked forward to this so much. I would schedule playdates with friends who had children that were similar in age. Finding my "tribe" of mommy friends really helped, too.

I was also gearing up to be the president of Junior League that summer, which really helped me with my identity. I was a mommy and a wife, but it was important to me to have other interests.

With everything I had going on, I wasn't giving the attention to my business that it needed. The time came to write my bid to renew my contract with the government and I knew it wasn't up to standard. The negative feedback on my proposal was completely accurate and fair. That was when I knew it was time to bless and release the business I had worked so hard at building all of those years.

The truth was, I was finding more fulfillment in spending time with Aidan. He was at a precious age where his eyes lit up and he smiled whenever he saw me. I still had my tearful moments, but I knew how to manage my feelings.

It was after about six months of counseling that I actually heard myself say out loud, "I think this thing is turning around."

CHAPTER 6

The Fork in the Road

By the time Aidan was a year and a half old, he had one speed. Fast. He ran everywhere with his arms up in the air. I spent so much time chasing him that I literally couldn't keep my pants on. I had lost weight from being "on the go." I didn't have time to buy jeans in a smaller waist size, so they were always sliding down my hips. My girlfriends teased me about it. I am sure that I was quite a sight for my neighbors as I chased Aidan down the sidewalk.

The mornings were our special cuddle time together in bed. I would sip my coffee and he would drink his milk while I read books and snuggled with him. I couldn't get enough of his thick, curly blond hair and his big blue eyes. Dirk and I were really enjoying being parents to our little Aidan. He was an observant and intelligent little boy, and every day there was a new milestone that fascinated us. He always made us laugh.

I started thinking about when it would be time to give Aidan a sibling, wanting our children to be close in age. I was five and a half years older than my sister. We were very close growing up, but once I became a teenager, our relationship was more disconnected. When I wasn't in school, I would be found waiting tables, taking voice lessons, and on the weekends, going dancing with my best friend, Sherry. My sister wanted to tag along, but our age difference didn't warrant it. Once she was in college, we grew close again.

Dirk was in a similar situation. He was four years younger than his youngest sibling and twelve years younger than his oldest. We knew early on that we wanted our children to be close in age, so I suggested to Dirk that it was a good time for us to get started on baby number two. As he often says, he was ready to "rock 'n' roll."

Life was crazy for us. We had just spent the last six months opening a restaurant, and the Junior League presidential baton had just been handed to me. Still, I was feeling settled and emotionally stable again. Now that I was a "hybrid" mom, I was more organized and had learned to make efficient use of my free time. So, the practice of "baby making" started back up.

We lived in the college town of Norman, Oklahoma—home of the University of Oklahoma—and the entire town was getting ready to drive to Dallas for the weekend for the most notorious college football rivalry in the South: OU/Texas. Half of the stadium would be filled with OU Sooner fans and the other half with Texas Longhorns. As I was packing my suitcase, Aidan whimpered, "Toe, toe." He was just learning to talk, but I was surprised by his word choice. He kept saying the word over and over again, which confused me. It was every mother's nightmare when I set him down on the floor and he wouldn't stand. He collapsed in my arms and I realized he had been trying to tell me his knee hurt, but he didn't know the word.

I took Aidan to the pediatrician immediately. He thought Aidan might have sprained his knee but cautioned me that if he became feverish or lethargic, we should go straight to the emergency room. All day long, I watched Aidan like a hawk and was hopeful it was just a sprain. By early evening, he was running a fever and not acting like himself. We were off to the hospital.

Aidan's illness was a bit of a mystery to the doctors. It was possible he had an infection in his knee joint, but there were other more serious possibilities like junior rheumatoid arthritis looming overhead as well. The severity of what he might have hit me when we got to his hospital room and there was a sign that said *QUARANTINE* posted to his door.

Aidan's knee was drained and a culture of the bacteria was taken. His body's response to an aggressive cocktail of IV antibiotics would tell the doctors what they needed to know. In the meantime, I devised a strategy to get us through his four-day hospital stay. I mean—can you imagine trying to contain a one-and-a-half-year-old to a bed with an IV? I bought a DVD player and a stack of Barney videos that Aidan grew to love. In between singing songs with him and the giant purple dinosaur all day, I began my discussions with God.

Dirk and I had not been to church since Aidan was born. We scheduled our days around his naps. Our weekends were about spending quality time, sleeping when Aidan slept, going to the family farm or to visit my parents.

I looked over at my sick little boy in his hospital bed and promised God that if He would heal him, we would go back to church.

Dirk had to be at work the next morning, so I sent him home to get some rest. I tucked into a chair that folded out into an uncomfortable bed. It was hard to sleep with the nurses coming in and out to take Aidan's vitals and switch out his fluids. He had trouble sleeping, too, since his arm was bandaged from the elbow down to his wrist to prevent him from tearing out his IV. His room didn't get quite dark enough, so I fashioned a blanket to go on the top of the crib. I was relieved when he finally dozed off.

In the morning there was no Dirk. It was completely unlike him to oversleep. After a few hours I began to worry and texted him. I received a reply from him that said, "Guess where I am?" I couldn't even begin to imagine where Dirk might be. He texted again. "I'm downstairs in the emergency room with a kidney stone. They just admitted me."

Life was getting very real, very quickly. Both of my boys were sick in the hospital at the same time. It was suddenly and unexpectedly my turn to be the "rock" of the family. I knew you weren't supposed to bargain with God for miracles, but I also knew firsthand that God made miracles happen.

I had been married for three months when I found out my mom had stage four colon cancer. I was absolutely devastated, and I immediately assumed the worst was going to happen. I called Dirk at work and hysterically screamed that I couldn't lose my mom. She was a retired schoolteacher and I knew she was going to be a loving and amazing grandmother to our children.

The following week, the results from her PET scan brought even worse news. The scan revealed spots on her liver and lymph nodes around her colon. She only had eighteen months to live. I didn't even pack a suitcase; I just got in my car and drove the two hours to my parents' home.

When I walked into their house, the magnitude and enormity of the situation had already set in with my dad. I found him sitting at the dining room table cradling his face in his hands. He had his quirks, but he loved my mom. My mom was in her bathroom wearing a nightgown, washing her face. She turned to me with the water still running and mustered up a smile. I hugged her and sobbed in her arms. She said to me in a very soft tone, "It's going to be okay." I squeezed her tightly. I didn't want to let her go.

My mom's colon resection surgery was the week before Thanksgiving. The morning of the surgery, Dirk and I gathered in her hospital room with my dad and my mom's mom, whom we called Gigi. She was a retired librarian and a very simple, sweet woman with the tiniest wrists and ankles I had ever seen. She was also the most faithful woman I had ever known. Before they wheeled my mom down the hall, we said a prayer for her. At the tail end of the prayer, Gigi spoke up: "Father, please don't let there be any cancer in her lymph nodes, her liver, or her colon. Please bind it up and make it disappear. We are asking for a miracle! Please, Father—take me instead. Don't take her. Her family needs her, Father. We pray for a miracle."

It was such an emotional moment. I was confused and angry that my sweet Gigi would pray for something so specific and miraculous when we already knew from the biopsies and PET scans that my mother had cancer in her liver and her lymph nodes. Why would she get my mom's hopes up right before the surgery?

The surgery was supposed to take in excess of four hours. I walked downstairs to center myself and get some coffee. Gigi stayed upstairs in the waiting room, reciting her prayer over and again. After a couple of hours, I headed back upstairs. Just as I sat down, the surgeon walked out, still in his blue scrubs and paper cap. He was shaking his head back and forth. I gulped and prepared myself for the bad news. Nobody was more surprised than I when he said, "It's a miracle."

My grandmother slumped over with relief as he continued, "We successfully removed the cancer from the colon; the resection was a success. The spots we saw on the liver appear to be only fatty spots, not cancer. One lymph node was swollen, but it doesn't appear to be cancerous either. She won't need chemo or radiation, as the cancer didn't penetrate the colon wall. She's nothing short of a miracle. I—I can't explain it."

Witnessing the specificity of my Gigi's prayer and the inexplicable healing of my mother forever changed the way I prayed. I learned to be specific in my prayer requests and to be unafraid in asking for things that defied science. I realized that I was not helpless; I was powerful in prayer. With this in mind, I prayed if not every hour, then at least every other hour for my boys. I woke up in the middle of night and prayed over Aidan, for his complete healing. As my sweet Gigi taught me, I look not at what our eyes see, but instead what our faith sees. I even prayed for the IV bag of antibiotics to kill the bacteria and make whatever virus Aidan had go away. I also prayed that Dirk would be restored by his procedure and be able to walk out of the hospital. I prayed for the Lord to transform both of my boys into radiant health.

That afternoon after his procedure, Dirk came up to his room and recuperated with us.

"I now know what it feels like to give birth," he said. I laughed.

The next day we knew Aidan was feeling better because he was starting to put weight on his leg. By the following morning, he was running down the halls with his rolling IV cart. I was incredibly relieved. I was so tired, not just from the lack of sleep but from the emotional aspects of our ordeal.

Thankfully, it was a nightmare with a happy ending. We were sent home that Sunday afternoon. I thought back to the previous Thursday night, when we didn't know if Aidan had an infection or a life-altering disease. I was so grateful.

U2 was playing at Memorial Stadium (where the OU Sooners played football) that night. They were one of our favorite bands and we had plans to go with a group of twenty friends. I was hesitant to leave Aidan home, but when both my mother and mother-in-law offered to stay with him and convinced us to go, I felt secure about leaving him for a few hours.

It was such a fun night—we needed it. We had been tested, brought closer as a family, and had been put on the right path.

CHAPTER 7

An Unseasonably Warm November

We started back to church the following Sunday. I had a new appreciation for life after Aidan's health scare. It felt great to be there and to reconnect with some friendly faces. Dirk and I had settled into our new Sunday routine and felt like we were "home."

Somehow—even in the shadow of such an emotional time—I had gotten pregnant!

"This is our little blessing," I thought as I saw the positive results on the digital pregnancy test. It felt extra special because of everything we had been through. I was so thankful it happened so quickly—we had only been trying for a month. I was on top of the world.

At four and a half weeks, I called Dr. Allison's office and scheduled my first appointment for the Tuesday before Thanksgiving. We had already told our parents and my sister I was pregnant. I was looking forward to going home to see my family and share the exciting news in person with my Gigi. I found myself daydreaming about our baby and wondering whether it was a boy or a girl. I loved the idea that Aidan and the baby would be so close in age. My imagination ran away with me as I pictured my large family. I knew Aidan would be a wonderful big brother.

Since this was our second child, I knew what to expect at the doctor's office that morning. A technician would perform a vaginal ultrasound and we would listen to that magical sound of our baby's heartbeat. It was slightly awkward when the technician came into the examination room where Dirk and I were waiting. The technician was a girl named Amy— a friend from Junior League. "It doesn't bother me, if it doesn't bother you," she said, as I placed my feet in the stirrups.

After having my vagina washed by a complete stranger in the hospital after having Aidan, I had no shame.

Dirk squeezed my hand as the machine came to life. I have to admit, it was a little embarrassing as she rolled the condom onto the probe and began the ultrasound. A low-grade hum filled the room as she moved the probe around trying to find our baby. I couldn't see the monitor, since it was facing her, but I knew at this stage, our little baby was probably about the size of a lentil.

Instead of the usual enthusiasm technicians are known for, she grew quiet once she had found the baby. Her freckled face grew still as she studied the monitor. My heart began to race when she rolled her stool away from the machine.

"I will be right back."

Dirk squeezed my hand again and maintained his usual calm demeanor. I immediately started praying. I wanted to know what was going on. What could the issue possibly be?

She was only gone for less than a minute, but it seemed like an eternity. She pushed her red hair away from her face as she sat back down on her stool. She spoke to us in a soft, reassuring manner.

"Here is what I'm seeing. At this stage, we normally hear a heartbeat. Maybe you're not as far along as you think you are. This is not atypical or uncommon, so I wouldn't worry too much. I want you to go home and enjoy the holiday weekend. We will see you in a week and I am sure we will find a heartbeat." She squeezed my hand and gave me a hug.

Suddenly, I was so grateful she had been my technician. What started off so awkwardly was now a blessing. I knew she had her own children, so she understood the gravity of this moment. She spoke to me like a friend.

I had a flash to the day Aidan was born. I remembered Dirk's words: "If this is the only child you can give me, it's okay." I hoped to God they weren't prophetic.

As I changed out of the cloth gown, I could feel the tension in my entire body. I wondered to myself how I could possibly relax, knowing our baby might not have a heartbeat. I had arrived at my appointment feeling on top of the world. I was proud of my family planning abilities, how quickly I had become pregnant, and the perfect age difference between Aidan and our second baby.

Now I was hit by the harsh, cold reality that I was not in control. This little baby that was inside of me, that I was already so connected to, might actually not survive. Dirk was more optimistic. "We'll go back next week and everything will be fine."

As we drove home I knew I didn't have just myself to think about. I was already a mother to an amazing little boy. I knew I had to put on my "mommy face" for him. It suddenly occurred to me that, just as I would never give up on Aidan, I needed to be a champion for this baby inside of me. In that moment, I realized it was a decision I needed to make. And so I chose hope. I had moments of worry, but I had to think positively.

On Thanksgiving morning, I woke up in my parents' guest room. It was so comforting to be there. They "collected" lots of things. My mom has saved *everything,* from her wedding mementos (which include every single receipt from their honeymoon) and *every single* item from my childhood and my sister's. From baby blankets, outfits, and clippings from our hair to our McDonald's Smurf glasses, Barbies, and vintage Fisher-Price toys—she kept it all. Bless her heart, she even made scrapbooks with photographs, clippings, and flyers from every one of my performances. My parents had lined their office walls with autographed photographs of every celebrity they had in their limos, including a shirtless Patrick Swayze and my mom posing with the Righteous Brothers in 1980.

As I got out of bed that Thanksgiving morning, Aidan was crying. I went into the room where he had slept, turned on the light, and picked him up. I sang him the "Good Morning" song I had been singing to him from the day he was born. We were the only two who were awake—the house was completely quiet. Taking care of Aidan was a very positive distraction. I wanted his days to be completely normal and for him to feel nothing but secure and loved.

Once my parents and Dirk were up, we all ate breakfast and watched the Macy's Thanksgiving Day Parade in our pj's. I tried to compartmentalize my thoughts and not think about what was going on inside my body. I knew that until Aidan went down for a nap, there was no space for my feelings. It was so confusing because I still had completely normal pregnancy symptoms. I was nauseous, tired, and had the same food aversions as when I was pregnant with Aidan. Yet there was the very real possibility that something was wrong with the baby. I reminded myself I had to hope for the best.

My mom and I spent the morning going back and forth to the kitchen to check on the turkey and the ham. Because my parents were in the limo business, things were always crazy at their home. They worked out of their house and answered their multiple cell phones twenty-four hours a day, seven days a week. When they said Thanksgiving lunch would be ready at one, I knew it would really be ready closer to three.

Dirk had gone to pick up Gigi from her house. She had recently started to get disoriented with her driving, so unless she was going only the short distance to the market, she relied on my mom for getting around. I had been looking forward to telling Gigi the news about my pregnancy in person. Even now, with the possible complications, I planned to share what was going on with her. She was the most faithful person I knew, and now more than ever, I needed her prayers.

My sister was out of town spending Thanksgiving with her new boyfriend, Andrew, and his family. When we finally sat down to eat, my dad's business cell phone rang right as Dirk began the prayer. My father jumped out of his chair.

"Everyone, hold on a minute."

He answered his cell phone, then ran into his home office. We all sat there waiting for him. Five minutes later he returned. He took a seat in his chair and placed his napkin back in his lap and chuckled as he raised his eyebrows. "You never know when money calls."

Once Chucky C. was settled in, Dirk finished the prayer. We went around the table expressing gratitude. I didn't want to make a big deal about what I was going through, so I didn't bring it up. Instead, I looked over at Aidan sitting in his high chair, who was already digging in to the mashed potatoes. I was so thankful for that little guy. I didn't say it out loud, but I was also thankful for my parents' chaos, which sometimes made me laugh. Today it was a welcomed distraction from all of my heavy feelings.

After lunch, I sat down with my sweet Gigi. She was wearing turquoise heirloom Indian jewelry, a typical polyester pastel pant outfit, and her SAS shoes. Her presence was so full of love and comfort. I laid my head in her lap and she stroked my hair. She smelled like a combination of Wrigley's spearmint gum and Avon perfume.

Gigi had been through so much—the Great Depression; my grandfather, Jack, going away to fight in WWII, followed by his hospitalization and shock therapy for depression when he was stationed in a different city as an Oklahoma Highway Patrolman. In 1993 he began his battle with dementia. He would roll over in bed at night and ask Gigi, "Who are you?"

"I am your wife of sixty years," she would reply.

His answers varied; sometimes he would smile, pat her, and say "Oh! I did pretty good, then. You're good looking!" Other times, he would argue with her that he wasn't married. That is when she started sleeping with a photocopy of their marriage license under her pillow, so she could "prove" she was supposed to be in his bed.

His caretaking really wore on Gigi, yet she stayed strong in her faith. She told me it was important to realize that life would be hard at times, and during those times it's important to persevere. She encouraged me to pray my way through it. She reminded me to always have hope. I should never give up hope. I felt so protected in her lap. I wanted to stay there forever.

On Friday, we drove out to the family farm to spend the day with my in-laws. The O'Haras are a big family and live all over the country, so our tradition is to get together on Thanksgiving and at the same time celebrate Christmas—creating a holiday we affectionately call "Thank-mas." After dinner, we opened Christmas gifts. It was one of the warmest Novembers I could remember, and it felt strange to open gifts when it was seventy degrees outside.

My sister-in-law Dena loves shopping, so she invited me to hit the stores on Saturday. I always loved spending time with her and my niece Natalie. Some retail therapy sounded like a good distraction, so we decided to meet at the mall the next morning.

The mall was in full swing. Christmas music played over the crowds of murmuring shoppers. Families lined up in a queue that stretched a hundred yards for a "Photo with Santa." I could smell the Bath & Body Works holiday scents from the store up ahead. As we passed it and made our way toward the big fountain in the middle of the mall, I felt a strange pain in my abdomen. It lasted about fifteen seconds and went away. We kept walking.

A few minutes later it was back, stronger than the last time. I looked over at Dena.

"Something isn't right. I—I think I need to sit down for a minute."

I hadn't experienced anything like this in my pregnancy with Aidan, so it was very alarming. It didn't feel like menstrual cramps; it was more like a very mild contraction.

I sat down on a bench near the fountain. The pop-up kiosks selling everything from personalized Christmas tree ornaments to remote-controlled airplanes were all around me. I closed my eyes and took a few deep breaths, thinking maybe it would go away. After a few minutes, it subsided. I started to get up but as soon as I stood, the cramping came back immediately. This time the pain was heavier and more intense. I felt the panic surging through me as I turned to Dena, who had a look of grave concern on her face.

"I think I need to go home and lie down."

"Do you need for me to drive you?" Dena asked.

"No—thanks, but I will be okay. You guys have fun. I'll call you later."

I walked out of the mall as fast as I could. The tears started streaming down my face. I knew in my heart that something was horribly wrong. I felt like I was having a bad dream as I walked toward the sliding glass doors. My heart was racing—practically beating out of my chest.

I got onto the highway and drove the four miles back to my house. I was so torn emotionally. I was trying to keep my hope alive, but in the face of what was happening it was very difficult. My coping mechanism was always to imagine the worst-case scenario so I wouldn't be shocked later.

As soon as I walked in the door, I went straight to the bathroom. I looked down into the toilet and saw what I had been fearing: bright red blood. My face became extremely hot. I could hear my heartbeat in my ears. I went to lie down on our bed and called Dr. Allison. It was a holiday weekend, so I left a message with the answering service. Within five minutes she called me back.

"This is Dr. Allison. What's going on?"

I explained to her that I was cramping and bleeding. She didn't sound overly concerned, but she did give me doctor's orders to stay off of my feet and get some rest until my appointment on Tuesday.

My next phone call was to Dirk. He was still out at the farm with Aidan. I told him what was going on and that I would not be coming back to the farm that day. This wouldn't come as a big surprise to any of the O'Haras. After dinner on Thursday, when Aidan and the other grandkids weren't around, Dirk and I shared that I was pregnant but hadn't heard a heartbeat at our last appointment.

I usually enjoyed the long Thanksgiving weekend, but this year it seemed endless. Time was standing still. Tuesday couldn't come fast enough. Everything was completely out of my hands and my control. My thoughts vacillated between a determination to remain hopeful and a fearful despair. It was completely confusing and exhausting.

On Sunday morning, Dirk and Aidan went to church and the farm without me. I spent the day at home, resting and worrying by myself. I mused over the irony that we had gone back to church after Aidan and Dirk's health crises and now we had mine to contend with. I also wondered if God had in part nudged us to go back to church to prepare me to able to handle what might be a miscarriage. Whatever the case, I was glad we had our faith to lean into right now.

It was no secret I had "white coat syndrome." Every time I went to the doctor, my vitals were high because I was so anxious. It was no different at my appointment that Tuesday. There was so much wrapped into this one appointment that it was almost impossible to stay calm. I removed my pants, climbed up onto the table, and slid my feet into the stirrups.

Instead of a technician, we saw Dr. Allison this time. Dirk and I held hands as she performed a transvaginal ultrasound. Except for the hum of

the machine, the room was completely silent. Dr. Allison was uncharacteristically quiet. There were no words exchanged between us as she studied the monitor. Finally, she spoke.

"Here's the uterus sac and the fetus. I'm measuring you at seven and
a half weeks."

A woman knows her body better than anyone, so I was very sad but
not shocked when the doctor added, "I'm not seeing a heartbeat. I'm so
sorry." I turned to Dirk and we had a moment before Dr. Allison gently
outlined next step options for me.

"It's hard to say how long it's been since the baby stopped growing.
You can miscarry naturally or I can induce you. You can also do a D&C."

Wait, what? I had a sick feeling in my stomach as I got dressed. I
had been prepared for the worst and now that the worst had happened,
it was shocking. Knowing that our baby had passed away inside of me
was very, very hard. There was a part of me that wanted the baby removed
as soon as possible, but another part of me wanted to hang on and love it
as long as I could.

CHAPTER 8

A Strange Sense of Deja Vu

I was disoriented the moment Dirk and I stepped outside of Dr. Allison's office. It was seventy degrees and the winds, which were always strong, were blowing warm. They whipped up my hair and brought my struggle to the surface. I sobbed right there in the parking lot.

We were in unfamiliar territory. Dirk hugged me tight and told me he loved me. I got into the car. I was terrified to miscarry naturally, but was also scared about choosing surgery. I didn't dream this is what I would do when I left Dr. Allison's office.

An hour later, I walked into the lab to have my blood drawn for the surgery. The waiting room was packed. As I stood in line to check in at the registration desk, a torrent of thoughts flooded my mind. It was finally my turn to check in. My voice sounded as weak and battered as I felt.

"Um—I'm here for blood work."

The woman behind the desk vaguely looked up at me. "Can you speak up?" Her sharp voice made me feel like just another number. I could barely get the words out of my mouth as I handed her the paperwork for my D&C. "It's my first one. I'm sorry. I'm very emotional."

The woman surprised me by jumping out of her seat, coming around the desk and taking me to a private room. I cried and cried while they preregistered me. The technician who did my blood work was very sweet and apologized when he saw why I was there. For some reason this made me cry even harder.

I was there for a total of two hours. After the blood draw, they did an EKG test to ensure my heart was healthy enough to undergo anesthesia. I passed, and they sent me on my way.

Once I left the lab, it was time to switch back into my "mommy gear" and pick up Aidan from daycare. On the way home, we stopped and picked up food so I wouldn't have to worry about cooking dinner. At home, Aidan and I cuddled on the couch. We stayed there for hours. This experience made me realize how much a miracle babies really are, and how fortunate I was to have him. I had a deeper appreciation for him and cherished his very existence.

Later that night, my mom rolled in with enough clothing to stay for the better part of the week. I was so relieved. Her mere presence had a calming effect on me. We all want our moms in times like these.

I had a strange sense of déjà vu when Dirk and I got up in the dark the next morning. I had fasted overnight and was being driven to the hospital to have a baby taken from inside me. This time, the surgery would not result in us returning home a few days later with our baby in our arms. Today, they were taking away something we loved—even though we had never met.

It was a surreal drive. I was so anxious and overwhelmed with feelings of dread. I looked out at the street lamps, buildings, and other cars outside the window—it was as if they had a haunting, dreamlike quality. I hadn't slept much, maybe three hours total. My mind scrolled all night. I had turned on the television hoping it would distract my thoughts from the surgery that loomed ahead, but it hadn't.

The hospital was quiet and still. I had a sour pit in my stomach as we walked past the darkened coffee shop to the same registration desk as the day before. I could tell Dirk didn't really know what to say, so he concentrated on taking care of me and on being calm. He stayed behind in the waiting area while I followed the nurse to the pre-op room. My anxiety was high as I filled out more paperwork and responded to a series of questions I had already answered the day before.

Once the nurse had inserted the needle for the IV into my arm, she left the room. She returned shortly, with Dirk right behind her. I had already changed into the standard issue blue and white floral hospital gown and those horrid institutional socks with sticky soles. As instructed, I had also removed my wedding ring. I felt naked without it. The room was freezing cold.

Just seeing Dirk made me feel calmer. My heart was pounding and my breathing was shallow. He took a seat in the chair next to my hospital bed and took my hand. I was so ready to get this procedure over with. Having him sitting there so attentively was the only reason I could breathe. I told him over and over again how sorry I was that my body had failed us. He told me to stop saying such a thing.

Hearing the "bing" of the heart rate on the monitor made me even more nervous and perpetuated my anxiety. The nurse and I finally decided that some sort of sedative was in order. After about fifteen minutes, I felt woozy, warm, and relaxed like I had a couple of martinis. I welcomed it. By the time the nurse anesthetist came back to ask me even more questions, I was officially intoxicated.

Finally it was time. I looked over at Dirk, and he kissed me. Tears rolled down my face as two surgical nurses wheeled me down a sterile white hallway to the operating room. It was just like a scene out of a movie. Dr. Allison was in her surgical scrubs and mask waiting for me. She patted me on the shoulder.

"Everything will be fine."

The sound of my amplified heartbeat made me so nervous. The nurse anesthetist hovered over me and asked me to count backward from five. I counted down to three before drifting off.

I woke up hours later in an alcove that was partitioned with a curtain. My eyes were heavy and I was groggy. When I could finally focus, I saw another sweet friend from Junior League, Julie, standing in front of me wearing hot-pink scrubs, holding crackers and a can of Sprite. It was such a relief to wake up and see a familiar face. It was the very first time since I had gotten the sad news about my pregnancy that I was able to take a deep breath and exhale. Even though I was sad, I was so relieved it was over.

Julie had seen my name on the list of patients for the day and requested me. I was so thirsty I could hardly speak. High from the pain meds, I started my drunk talk. "Julie, you're my aaaaaa-ngel. I just love you so muccch . . . thank you for being here for me. . ." I held on to Julie's hand and patted it several more times as I came out of the anesthesia. Sprite and cracker mush drooled down my chin, but Julie was so sweet to me.

Once I was completely awake, Julie went to get Dirk. He took my belongings out of the plastic hospital bag and helped me get dressed. I wanted to get out of the hospital. I wanted my bed. I wanted to hold Aidan.

It was standard protocol for me to be taken out to our car in a wheelchair. When I got outside, the winds were blowing again. As I climbed into our SUV, they thrashed my hair around just as they had two days before.

CHAPTER 9

Pedaling Along

Within two hours of leaving the hospital, my thighs were absolutely screaming. I was in excruciating pain, despite being drugged up. The pain was unbearable. After a couple of hours I began to worry I had a blood clot. I found the number for the recovery center of the hospital and decided to call. A very sweet older nurse answered the phone and listened to my complaint.

"I just had a D&C this morning, and . . . I'm in so much pain. My thighs are just killing me, even though I am already on painkillers."

"Well, honey, your legs were strapped down to the table during the procedure. It is most likely from that. You were put into a frog position."

This was not the response I was expecting. I assumed I would be given a more technical answer.

That it came down to something so simple cracked me up. I thought about myself lying there unconscious in a frog position—for all of the surgical staff to see. I remembered that I hadn't "groomed" myself down there in weeks. I couldn't help but laugh.

"Are you serious? Well . . . that must have been a sight!" I said.

The nurse laughed a bit, which made me laugh harder. Dirk and my mom looked at me in complete confusion as to why my conversation about my D&C could possibly be funny. When I hung up the phone and explained it to them, they laughed with me for about fifteen minutes.

It felt good to laugh, but I also felt guilty.

My body was dumping hormones, so I was filled with all kinds of emotions. Ironically, I had awakened from the anesthesia angrier about my loss than I had been before the surgery. I tortured myself with questions that I couldn't answer. I couldn't help wondering if the baby was a boy or a girl. Was it genetically abnormal, or was there just something wrong with my body?

I spent the next three days curled up in bed in my flannel pj's. I continued to cramp and bleed and kept a heating pad on my stomach. My thighs continued to throb for two straight days. I felt so blessed to have my mom around. I think she enjoyed taking care of us.

The bleeding was lighter with every day that passed, but I was shocked at how much blood there was to begin with. I had only been seven or eight weeks pregnant, so the baby would have only been the size of a tadpole. Yet, the volume of blood was astonishing to me.

As much as I tried focusing on other things during the day, the blood was a constant, haunting reminder of the baby we had lost. I dreaded going to the bathroom, and every time I did, I couldn't help but have morbid thoughts about the clots and tissue that was once my baby. I tried as much as I could not to judge myself for all of the feelings I was having. I had friends who went through miscarriages and felt the same way I did. It was a huge loss, and it took them time to grieve and recover from it. There were other friends who chose not to share their miscarriages or D&Cs with anyone and didn't feel the need to grieve. There was no right or wrong. I reminded myself that every woman is different. We all show strength and vulnerability at different times and in different ways.

Spending time with Aidan was the highlight of my day. It was the best medicine and the only thing that could truly comfort me. He was just short of two and was obsessed with John Deere tractors and his Barney videos. I loved it when he would crawl up into bed with me to watch his videos.

"Mommy, hold you."

This was my cue to take his little outstretched arms and snuggle him up in mine. I couldn't help but hug him a little tighter, and every night when I rocked him to sleep after reading him stories, I saw him for the miracle that he was.

I kept work phone calls to a minimum while I was on bed rest. After about three days it was time to get back on my regular schedule. My employees at the restaurant had no idea what was going on with me personally, so the work texts and emails just kept coming.

After ten days the bleeding finally stopped, but my feelings lingered. I was really angry that this had happened. I felt slighted spiritually and I wanted to know what had caused this.

In some ways it was good to be back to "normal"—but I was not the same person. I could feel that the experience had changed me. I had so many questions and felt like I was missing something from my heart.

With Christmas around the corner, I made a choice to get into the holiday spirit. Aidan was at an age at which he understood the concept of Santa Claus. We wanted to make it special for him. My family wanted to come celebrate with us so they could be part of the fun with Aidan.

I went completely overboard decorating the whole house. It was beautiful, if I do say so myself. Our tree was in the front living room with beautifully wrapped gifts underneath it. We don't use the living room often enough, but at Christmas it becomes my happy place. This year was no different. Dirk started a fire in the fireplace for me, and I climbed into one of our black leather recliners with a blanket. I just stared at the sparkling lights of the tree.

On Christmas Eve my parents and my sister rolled in looking like the Griswold family from *Christmas Vacation*. They had tons of luggage, their cell phones, briefcases, and of course loads of gifts. My father was wearing one of his shirts with a wild print, and beneath the shirt was a gold chain with crucifix that he had not taken off since 1970. As soon as he walked in our door, he asked me to make him his favorite drink—a Shooter—which meant a vodka martini on the rocks.

"Make it a nice pour, Stephie."

Gifts are the love language of my family, and this year was no exception. After dinner we all gathered around the tree. Aidan was so excited to open his gifts. They were all John Deere themed, of course. This was his latest obsession. He would open each gift, squeal, and say, "Wook!"

Even in the middle of our family Christmas gift exchange, I knew there was no chance my father would hesitate to answer his limo company phones, which were forwarded to his cell phone. Between calls, he said to me and my sister, "Okay, girls, I got something for the two of you that I think you are really going to like." He had gone to a local boutique and bought us sequined dresses that were clearly meant for someone ten years younger than we were.

"I figured you could wear this on stage, Steph, and Mel, you can wear yours when you are out on a hot date with Andrew."

Melanie and I looked at each other and laughed, rolling our eyes.

The dresses were not anything my sister and I would ever wear, but I appreciated my father trying to show love and support. One of the gifts I opened from my sister was a gorgeous black leather designer wallet. Mel was still in her twenties, so I was really surprised by the extravagance of the gift. She had just started a new job and hadn't been able to be there when Aidan and Dirk were hospitalized or when I had my D&C.

"Mel, it's way too much!"

Tears were rolling down my little sister's cheeks. "Well, you've had a really tough year. You deserve it!"

We both laughed and hugged one another. By the time we were finished with the gifts, my father had surprisingly only taken three phone calls, which was a Christmas miracle in itself. After our gift exchange, it was time to get Aidan ready for bed. He was so excited about Santa coming and was hopeful he might see him. We set out a plate of cookies for Santa and carrots for his reindeer. While Aidan slept, Dirk and I put together Aidan's big gift. I also prepped the tenderloin for Christmas lunch. It was exhausting, but so much fun.

In the morning, Aidan's eyes lit up when he saw the gifts from Santa under the tree. His big gift from Santa was a John Deere pedal tractor. He even forgot all about the plate of cookies and the carrots, which had been gobbled up by Santa and his twelve reindeer. He got on the tractor and headed for the front door.

Even though it was freezing cold, we all went outside in our pajamas and watched Aidan pedal his tractor down the sidewalk. We joked that Santa could have brought Aidan an electric tractor, but he must have known that toddlers have plenty of energy to burn.

A flood of emotions came over me as we watched Aidan pedal up and down the sidewalk. I laughed at all of us standing in our driveway at six-thirty in the morning in our pajamas and robes. I felt so blessed as I looked at Aidan's sweet face and his enormous grin. His little feet could hardly reach the pedals.

Mel was right. It had been a rough couple of months. I thought back to just one month before, when I was still pregnant. So much had changed in those four weeks. On the positive side, I was more appreciative of every-one in my family—especially Aidan, who was the best big gift from Santa I could have ever asked for.

CHAPTER 10

The Garden of Life

After my miscarriage and D&C, I had retreated. Except for spending time with my two closest friends, Melissa and Stacy, I didn't socialize much. Stacy and Melissa are my "besties." They are like my sisters. Because of our long history together, I felt completely comfortable being vulnerable with them. They were like my favorite blanket I could snuggle up into without having to talk or answer any questions.

When Stacy and Melissa came over, I didn't fret about what the house looked like and I didn't worry about doing my hair or putting my makeup on. There was zero judgment among the three of us. The fact was, I didn't want to hang out with friends who were pregnant or had newborn babies—and there were a lot of them. It was hard for me to be happy around them because it reminded me of what I had lost.

Melissa was no stranger to loss. In 1995, she had survived the Oklahoma City bombing. She was in the Journal Record Building right across from the Murrah Federal Building, and at 9:02 that morning she happened to be standing behind a column that miraculously shielded her from devastation. She stood there and watched as in an instant, co-workers in the same hallway were swept away by the blast.

I met Melissa, who was a college friend of Dirk's, in 2001. She happened to be dating Ben, a close friend of mine from back home, so we seemed destined to meet. We immediately had great "friendship chemistry." She was everything Dirk had said she was—incredibly smart, successful, a fun spirit, and a great storyteller. Dirk and I were so excited when she and Ben got engaged after just six months of dating.

About a year later, Melissa introduced what became known as her "party hat" into our friendship. It was a straw cowboy hat that she wore when she was ready to turn off her work brain and play on the weekends. Even when she wasn't wearing it, the party hat was always in tow. Whether it was at my gigs or just a night on the town, when she put it on her head it was a signal to turn it up and have fun!

I had met Stacy at a Junior League meeting years ago. She was a petite blonde with a pretty freckled face and big brown eyes. She was very intelligent, sweet, and had a volunteer's heart. She was also an engineer, so she was very analytical and organized. I found out that Stacy had a birthday coming up in just a few days. Right before our Junior League meeting that week, I stopped off at the MAC Cosmetics counter and picked up a birthday present for her—a pink lip gloss called "Angel." Even though giving a gift to an acquaintance might come off as stalker-ish, I knew in my heart we were supposed to be friends. I had gone from knowing so many people in my hometown to living in a new community where I didn't have many girlfriends. I was willing to go out on a limb. I walked over to her and handed her the black shopping bag before the meeting started.

"Hey, it's your birthday next Monday, so I thought I would get you a little something."

Stacy opened the bag, then stared at me like I was from outer space. *Oh my gosh, she thinks I'm completely crazy*, I thought to myself as the meeting started.

It turned out Stacy did think I was a little crazy and had gone home and told her fiancé about my weird gesture. Rennie (whose personality is like mine—social and outgoing) encouraged her to pursue the friendship. The next day I received a text from her: "Thanks again for the lip gloss. Want to grab a glass of wine after the Junior League meeting next week?"

We grabbed dessert and champs (what we call champagne in the South) and laughed all night. We immediately became best friends. A year later, she and Rennie intentionally moved onto our street, then eventually became our next-door neighbors. We started doing everything together—trips, cookouts, and celebrating holidays. We were even pregnant together at the same time.

Stacy and Melissa knew better than anyone else (except for Dirk) what I was going through, and what I needed. They rallied around me in a way that only best friends know how.

With our lives so interconnected, it's hard to imagine how different my life would have been without the girls around. I probably would have laughed less and cried more without them. Even in the worst of times, I could always count on Melissa to slip on the party hat and for Stacy to bring the champs.

CHAPTER 11

Truly Adulting

My jaw dropped when my little sister called to tell me she had gotten engaged. It was early evening. I was on the highway headed to the restaurant and I almost wrecked as I screamed.

"But—she's so young!" I said to Dirk after I got off the phone with her.

"Steph, she's thirty," Dirk said.

"But, we will have to split up holidays with her now . . . we won't see her as often!"

Truthfully, I was so happy for her and her now fiancé, Andrew, but the depth of my reaction took me by surprise.

I was five and a half years old when Melanie was born. I could still vividly remember Gigi taking me to the hospital to see my newborn baby sister. She pulled up a step stool to the nursery window and pointed her out to me.

My parents had the same reaction to my sister's engagement when I spoke to them later on that day. Mel was the baby of our family, and we were so used to having her at every single holiday. We were a small family—it was always just us.

That night, as Dirk and I ate at our restaurant, I was flooded with memories of Melanie. When she was little, she had these beautiful big blue eyes, pigtails with ribbons, and the cutest little lisp. Growing up, we primarily entertained ourselves listening to records and singing. We spent hours making our own "music videos" and would dress up, practice, and lip sync to songs by Madonna, Weird Al, and Tina Turner while our dad videoed us.

Melanie's engagement ushered in a new era for us. She had been dating Andrew for two years, and he was a great addition to the family. I was excited to finally have a brother—a former college football player no less. Still, the milestone was a sure sign that we were, as I like to say, "truly adulting" now.

Because Melanie and I both like to do things in a *big* way, it came as no surprise that she had her heart set on marrying Andrew in the same church where Dirk and I had gotten married. Since I was a member of that church, she asked me to call to see if I could work some magic. I imagined that like most brides, Melanie would want the better part of a year to plan her wedding, but when I called the church office, I found out they had only one date available that year—and it was just six months away.

The months flew by and before we knew it, July had arrived. It was a hundred and ten degrees on the day of the wedding, but Melanie was not to be outdone by the weather. With her beautiful blonde hair, big smile, and infectious southern charm, she looked like something out of *Vogue*. In keeping with her larger-than-life personality, she walked down the aisle with our dad to a procession of stately trumpets.

It was a sentimental day for all of us for so many reasons. Aidan was her ring bearer and Gigi was in a wheelchair because of the stroke she had suffered a few months earlier. Even though she was paralyzed on one side of her body, she inspired all of us with her strength.

The reception was filled with our cousins, friends, Andrew's football buddies, and everyone in between. Melissa, Ben, Stacy, and Rennie were also invited, so it made the evening even more fun for Dirk and me. Early on, I got up on stage and sang Aretha Franklin's "Natural Woman" for my sister and Andrew. Aidan was two and a half now and had no fear. He wandered over to the stage in his tuxedo and stole the show by climbing up onto it with me and dancing to the song as I sang.

From the stage, I could tell this was going to be a fun night. I don't know if it was the extreme heat, but everybody was really letting their hair down and taking full advantage of the ice luge martini bar.

Even Dirk surprised me by lighting a cigar and letting loose. He normally had a couple of cocktails or beers but was never out of control. At one point on the dance floor, Ben stunned us by dropping down and doing the splits. We all guffawed at Bennie—who was stuck in that position until Rennie and Dirk pulled him up. Ben winced in pain.

"I think one of Ben's testicles just shot across the dance floor," Dirk said.

We all burst out laughing.

Around midnight, it was time for the party to move to Melanie and Andrew's hotel suite. Melissa, Stacy, and I grabbed our hubbies and piled into one of the limos waiting outside. When we pulled up to the hotel, Ben staggered out of the limousine and almost fell down. It might have been the effects of the ice luge martini bar or maybe his moves on the dance floor, but in either case, he was definitely done for the night.

When the elevator doors closed, I pushed "PH" for the penthouse suite, where the after-party was. Melissa took Ben to bed and joined up with us later. Stacy and Rennie had their own plan in mind and pushed "10" so they could go to their room. Stacy had a mischievous look on her face and let the words float out of her mouth like a soprano hitting a high note.

"I'm ovulating!"

As soon as the elevator doors opened onto the tenth floor, Dirk turned to Rennie and gave him several enthusiastic fist pumps.

"Go get it, Rennie!" Dirk said.

CHAPTER 12

The Luck of the Irish

About a month later, on a sweltering hot summer morning, the text alert on my phone chimed. I had just gotten out of the shower. On Saturdays my routine was always to have a little "me time," as I called it. You know—I would drink a hot cup of coffee in bed while I watched a cooking show; check my email and read Facebook; take a long shower, and actually shave my legs.

Saturdays were also reserved for my special outing with Aidan to our local farmers' market. We began the tradition when he was just one and a half. I wanted Aidan to meet the farmers and see where our food came from. I usually bought extra fruit and vegetables and dropped them on Stacy's doorstep right next door.

The text alert on my phone chimed again. It was Stacy. Her message read, "Call me ASAP." I immediately picked up the phone and called her. She giggled when she answered the phone.

"I'm pregnant!"

I laughed and shrieked with excitement, "Awww, a souvenir from Melanie's wedding."

I could not have been more thrilled for Stacy. She was my best friend and my next-door neighbor. Stacy and Rennie were loving parents to their two-year-old daughter, Ainsley, and deserved all the happiness in the world.

As I hung up the phone with her, I could feel other weird emotions swirling around inside of me—that I would never want anyone else to know about. It felt so terrible that even identifying the feelings in my mind was jarring: I was a little envious of my best friend. Okay, I was actually *very* envious.

Wandering around the farmer's market with Aidan, I was not proud of how I was feeling. I also didn't know what to do with it. Here I was full of jealousy. In any other case, it would have been Stacy I would have gone to for advice. I would have poured two glasses of wine, marched right on into her house, and plopped down on her couch for some girl talk. Today was different. I knew I needed to put what I was feeling aside and celebrate with my friend.

A week later, Dirk and I were having Melissa, Ben, Stacy, and Rennie and their kids over for a cookout. We made a point of doing it a couple of times a month. Aidan loved playing with their kids. The husbands watched preseason football shows outside while monitoring the grill. Along with the hamburgers, I had also bought a bottle of champagne so that we could toast Stacy and Rennie's pregnancy over dinner.

When I got up that morning, I was a bit nauseous. I also noticed that my boobs were quite a bit larger than normal. I thought about a box of leftover pregnancy tests I had in the cupboard. My mind raced as I considered taking one.

"Why not?"

I was literally on the edge of my seat as I watched the faint blue line of the pregnancy test darken. I was in complete shock. I was pregnant! Just to be sure, I did a second test. The positive results were immediate. I was still in disbelief, so I even took a digital test. It was positive too!

I lined up all of the tests on the bathroom counter and stared at them for a minute or two. My heart was pounding with excitement. I thanked God over and over for this second chance. I laughed at how thrilled I would be at not being able to have a glass of champagne later at dinner.

Dirk was in the family room playing with Aidan and his cars and trucks. I cuddled up to him and told him in a soft voice that I was pregnant. He was genuinely happy and reassured me that this time everything would be okay. Aidan wasn't paying attention and was too young to understand what we were talking about anyway. Given our last experience, we decided not to tell him anything. I did call my mom to share our news with her.

"It will all work out this time. Just think positively!"

Stacy, Rennie, and Ainsley were always the first to arrive, since they lived right next door. I pulled Stacy aside as soon as she walked in the door. I had been daydreaming all day long about the two of us being pregnant together the way my mom and my aunt had been. It was a very special time and it had created a unique bond between them. I held Stacy's hands and jumped up and down like a giddy schoolgirl.

"Guess what? I'm pregnant!"

Stacy's mouth dropped. "What? Are you serious?" She was overjoyed. She smiled and her eyes welled up with tears. She laughed and said, "Oh, hormones!"

Not long after, Melissa walked in wearing her infamous red Crocs. Her two boys immediately ran outside to play on the new swing set with Aidan and Ainsley. Melissa knew about Stacy's pregnancy, but not mine. I intentionally hadn't set out the champagne flutes so she would have to ask me for them. When I told her we would only need one glass, for her, she was immediately on to me.

"Oh my God. You're pregnant, aren't you?"

Stacy came over and gave me a big hug. The three of us went down the dreamy path together. We decided she was having another girl and that I was having another boy. We joked about what their personalities would be like and imagined that when they were teenagers they would sneak out of our houses and become each other's first kiss.

When we sat down to dinner, we shared our pregnancy news with

Ben and Rennie. We joked about the blessings of the ice luge at my sister's wedding. Rennie also led a prayer thanking God for our friendship and for bringing us all together. Then he thanked God for our simultaneous pregnancies and asked for protection over them. That our pregnancies would be healthy, go full term, and yield happy, healthy babies. After the prayer, Melissa raised her glass and offered a toast to Stacy and me.

"Cheers to my two friends who can't enjoy the champs with me."

As I stood up to clear the table, that cramping I had felt as I walked around the mall after Thanksgiving returned.

"No."

"No, God. Please."

I tried to stay calm as I dropped the plates on the kitchen counter and headed straight for the bathroom. I pleaded with God as I sat down on the toilet.

"Please God. Not again. I am begging you."

I looked down and saw bright red blood swirling in the toilet bowl, just as it had seven months before.

The sight of it was devastating. I started sobbing. I was so angry and confused. It was heartbreaking to know that the little baby inside of me, whom I had already grown to love, was gone just like that.

As I sat there crying, I wondered who I should be mad at. My body? God? This was now the second time this had happened. Was there something wrong with me? Was Aidan going to be an only child?

I was having so many thoughts and feelings. I was also embarrassed and ashamed. Here I had taken my two best friends and their husbands, whom I loved and cherished, on this emotional ride during dinner. I wasn't sure what to do now. Should I go back out and act like everything is fine? Or do I tell everyone the truth, knowing it would make them all feel awkward and ruin our beautiful evening?

After putting on a pad and taking some Advil, I mustered up the strength to go back out there. Everything felt like it was in slow motion. The tree frogs were singing as the kids ate popsicles on the swing set. Coldplay was on the Sonos speakers.

I felt suffocated by the humidity as I motioned to Dirk to come inside to the kitchen.

"I'm miscarrying again." My voice was high pitched—trying to keep from crying.

I could tell Dirk was shocked, but was trying as best as he could to hide it.

"Are you sure?"

"Yes, I'm bleeding heavily. I know it."

Right or wrong, I felt that I was disappointing Dirk. My mind flashed back to him on bended knee, proposing to me and asking me to have his five children. I collapsed into his arms and cried, and just as I had the morning of my D&C, I apologized to him. He held me in his arms.

"I'm so sorry. I know I am disappointing you."

"Stop saying that."

Melissa and Stacy came in and sat down at our dining room table. Stacy lifted up her hair to cool off her neck.

"It's too hot out there. I'm getting nauseous."

They both noticed the black mascara tears streaking down my face. Stacy looked very concerned.

"What's wrong?"

I couldn't help but bawl.

"I went to the bathroom and I'm miscarrying."

Their jaws dropped. All of the air was sucked out of the room.

Melissa came over and put her arms around me. "I'm so sorry."

Within five minutes, everyone was gone. On her way out the door,

Melissa said, "We're going to get out of your hair. You need peace and quiet right now." Ben and Rennie both gave me comforting pats on the back as they walked past me. As I closed the door behind our friends, I felt like I was closing the door on the world. I felt isolated in my reality, where I could only focus on the fact that I was miscarrying.

Dirk put Aidan to bed that night. I was up several times during the night, in and out of the bathroom. The cramps were as severe as they had been back in November, when I miscarried the first time. I was bleeding heavily and passing blood clots. It was *complete* agony.

The next day I spoke with Dr. Allison. She explained that I had probably had a chemical pregnancy (which occurs when the fertilized egg does not attach itself to the uterine wall). These usually happen within a week or two of a missed period. She asked me if I wanted to consider another D&C, but I said no. She told me chemical pregnancies were very common and not to worry about it. I was due for my yearly exam in just a couple of months.

"We'll talk about it when you come in for your annual."

Despite her reassurance, I was scared. True to my nature, I started to focus on the worst-case scenario. "What if this is my thing—recurrent miscarriages?" The next week was excruciating physically and mentally. Although I had decided not to have another D&C, I was amazed at the volume of blood and tissue my body was passing for an embryo that was only a few weeks along. Every trip to the bathroom was a reminder of my loss.

In about a week, the physical part of the miscarriage was over, but the unbearable mental agony continued. I was thinking about it all the time. My mind would flash over and over again to Dirk in that pink and orange sunset, on bended knee, asking me to have his five children.

I was so confused. I wanted a big family, but it seemed possible that

I might not be able to deliver on the promise I made when I accepted his proposal.

Deep down I knew that Dirk loved me, but I also knew he didn't have a lot of experience with failure. He joked that he had the luck of the Irish, but the truth was he seemed to have been born knowing how to succeed. Even though I had my own accomplishments, I couldn't stop comparing myself to him and feeling like a disappointment.

A few weeks later, the stifling heat and humidity of the Oklahoma summer gave way to the crispness that comes with fall. For me, it was time to get back to wearing sweaters and celebrate the birthdays of five of my dearest friends. With a couple of exceptions, all of my besties had birthdays in September. We are notorious for pulling pranks and sending each other gag gifts on our birthdays, so it was time to start thinking up some good ones.

Dirk and I had shifted our focus away from trying to get pregnant again, so nobody was more surprised than I when I missed my period. I knew I had one pregnancy test left, so I tentatively went into our master bathroom and took it. I stared at the blue line that told me I was pregnant. Instead of being excited, I felt a pit of nervousness in my stomach. "What does this mean?" I wondered to myself. Would the third time be the charm, or would I miscarry again?

Dirk was in the family room reading the newspaper. I went over to him and shared my news. He crinkled the newspaper down, looked up at me, and smiled.

"That's awesome, honey." He gave me a hug and brushed my bangs out of my eyes.

I sensed his nervousness. It echoed my own. We decided that in the short term we would keep this pregnancy to ourselves to shield our families from the emotional roller coaster. It was hard enough being on it ourselves.

One minute I felt like I was desperately fluttering around trying not to worry. The next minute I was the voice of reason for myself.

"Wait, hang on. I'm pregnant. This baby inside of me deserves for me to have hope."

Forty-eight hours later I went to the bathroom and there was a tinge of blood on the toilet paper. The sight of it sent me spiraling. I could hear Dr. Allison's words: "We'll worry if it happens again." It was a pattern. I thought of one of my cousins, who had suffered several miscarriages. I wondered if I could have inherited the same condition.

Stacy and Rennie came over that night. The four of us sat on the couch in shock. Stacy was bawling. I was struggling to sort through my feelings. I felt like I was circling a drain.

"Can we please pray?"

We wrapped our arms around one another and Rennie recited a beautiful prayer. He asked God to take away my barrenness and to break the curse of infertility. I felt blessed to have these kinds of friends in my life who would do this with me.

I drifted in and out of sleep that night. I woke up feeling like a spider spinning frantically. I wanted to fix whatever was wrong with me, and I wanted to fix it now. I knew I needed to find somebody to talk to.

CHAPTER 13

Intercession

"I don't think she's for me," I thought to myself as I watched the expressionless face of my new counselor from the burgundy couch in her office. We had already gotten off on the wrong foot. She was running thirty minutes behind and now she was sitting at her desk looking at her computer screen as she did her intake on me. She didn't look at me or in my direction.

I was in complete darkness and I needed someone to start punching holes to let some light in. I had already tried talking to our church pastor, but it was the most awkward conversation I had ever had with anyone. In fact, I felt even worse after I hung up the phone with him.

I had first met our pastor almost eight years before, when my relationship with Dirk became serious. I moved into town and we started attending Sunday services together at the church Dirk had joined while he was in college.

The pastor was caring, warm, and made people feel comfortable. He would crack jokes and was very personable. I was very touched when he came to see Aidan during his hospitalization, even though we hadn't been to church in a while. He prayed over him and was of great comfort to Dirk and me.

After two chemical pregnancies, I was so confused—I didn't even know what to pray for. In addition to my emotional crisis, I was also experiencing a faith crisis. That's when I called our pastor for support. It was a Tuesday afternoon and I had just put Aidan down for a nap. Not one to beat around the bush, I jumped right in.

"Since you were so helpful and supportive during Aidan's hospitalization, I was hoping I could talk to you about an issue Dirk and I are facing. I've had a couple of miscarriages and I'm in a bit of a spiritual crisis. I was wondering if you have any advice for us—or maybe you could pray for us?"

The pastor who was known for being great one-on-one was suddenly stammering over his words.

"Oh, oh my. Gosh, wow. That's . . . that's just . . . oh, I'm sorry. You and your husband, you just have to pray."

It was so awkward that I was compelled to take over the conversation and talked a little in depth about our struggles. The pastor stumbled over a few more words, apologized, and then hung up. We were one and done.

It was obvious he had never been approached on the topic of miscarriage before. I regretted having called him. I realized I had been naïve thinking a man the same age as my father could have such a delicate conversation with a woman. His generation did not discuss infertility or miscarriage. These real-life issues were just swept under the rug.

I knew then that I would have to get my spiritual support somewhere else. I needed someone to help me process my feelings, and thought it should be a woman, so she would have empathy. I also wanted her to be a Christian, because I wanted advice from someone who could understand my spiritual struggle.

I had heard years before that God sometimes sends us angels in human form, so I closed my eyes and prayed. "Please, God. I cannot trudge through this on my own. I need intercession through people. Please bring women into my life that can help to direct and guide me."

Inasmuch as I felt like I was lost in a small boat, I knew God didn't want me to be passive. I got on the computer and Googled the words *Christian Counselor*. Three names came up on the screen. One of them had a picture of a woman who looked warm and approachable. Since I was a big believer in signs and her first name was *Angela,* I immediately called and scheduled an appointment.

I certainly didn't expect God to send a smiling angel with a halo and wings my way, but this was clearly *not* what I was expecting. The window of Angela's office was covered by a dark, closed shade, which created a very somber atmosphere. I really didn't like her demeanor and decided to give her another sixty seconds before getting up and leaving. Just as I had that thought, she grabbed a clipboard and came to sit across from me.

"Tell me your story."

My hands flailed as all of the emotions from the last two years poured out of me. "I'm having recurrent miscarriages, and my husband and I want five kids. God isn't listening to me and I feel like I'm being punished." Saying the words felt good and horrible all at once. Angela quietly listened to me for the next twenty minutes, then finally spoke.

"I think you have very low self-esteem, Stephanie."

Her observation was like a splash of cold water on my face. I was here to talk about my miscarriages—and she was judging my self-esteem. I was confused.

"Why do you say that?"

"The way you were waving your hands when you spoke. That's indicative of low self-esteem."

As much as I didn't want to dig up my history, I had to admit she had homed in on something.

"Yeah, I don't feel good about myself at all."

Angela smiled at me. "I think you have the gift of self-awareness. Not everybody does. I want to help you develop tools that will build your self-esteem."

We didn't discuss my miscarriages or fertility issues, but when the session ended, I had a better understanding of myself and my feelings of failure. These were old feelings left over from my younger years. Now they were back again.

I wasn't convinced that Angela was in fact one of my angels, but she had given me some exercises to do at home, and some scriptures to read. I was supposed to reflect back on all of the times when I felt I wasn't good enough or that I had failed, and write them down. She asked me to bring them to the next appointment. I didn't know if I would make it to our next appointment, but I knew I didn't want to start over with someone else. The only thing I was certain about was that this was *not* going to be an easy or quick fix.

CHAPTER 14

Just a Season

It was hard to believe it was almost a year since we had given Aidan his John Deere pedal tractor for Christmas. In eleven months, he had become deft at maneuvering the tractor and its four-foot trailer up and down the sidewalk in front of our house. He was quite a sight—he would dress head to toe in John Deere gear. The kid was a walking, talking advertisement for their children's Christmas catalog. He pedaled back and forth on the sidewalk for hours on end. People would slow their cars down and honk when they saw him. Aidan would smile and wave at them and pedal faster to show off. It always made me laugh.

One chilly afternoon I was bundled up in my coat out in front of our house watching Aidan. Stacy pulled into her driveway and hopped out of her car with Ainsley in tow. She was about four months pregnant now and even though she was wearing a winter coat, her belly was starting to show. For some reason, it was a shock for me to see her baby bump. I was happy for her, but couldn't help thinking about myself and how far along I would have been in my pregnancy. Seeing her filled me with both excitement for her and lots and lots of envy. I felt horrible for feeling that way.

Normally, we would have made chitchat and caught up on the day's events—but today was a little uncomfortable. Our friendship was still solid, but for the past few months I had been so emotional that I had minimized seeing Stacy. We texted several times a day, but actually seeing her was a constant reminder of what could have been for me. I could tell Stacy knew what I was feeling that day, so after a quick hello we both went into our houses.

I knew it was time for us to have a conversation. I left Aidan with Dirk, walked the fifty feet to her house, and knocked on her glass front door. I could see her sitting on her couch watching one of the reality shows she turned on to relax after work. I waved to her through the door and let myself in. She turned off the television as I settled myself onto the couch with her.

"Hey—so . . . I know that this is weird for both of us. I want you to know that I truly am happy and excited for you. Seeing your baby bump for the first time did remind me of how far along I would have been. And it does make me a little sad. But as hard as it is for me, you're my bestie and are having a baby and we need to celebrate that."

Stacy teared up a bit. "I know. I just feel so bad that things didn't work out for you."

I saw then that this was just as hard on her as it was on me.

"There are going to be moments that are hard for me, but I want to celebrate your pregnancy."

I reached over and gave Stacy a hug. Dirk and I were happy for her and she was sad for us. I put my hand on her belly and whispered to the baby.

"Aunt Steph loves you."

I felt lighter when I left Stacy's house. I knew I would still have my moments, but counseling was allowing me to be heard and validated. I still wasn't entirely convinced that Angela was one of my angels. She was very serious, and even after a month of seeing her, it seemed that she never blinked or smiled. But she was teaching me that I was entitled to my feelings. Loss was loss. My experience was as valid as anyone else's. Just as important, I was learning from Angela how to manage my feelings and talk about them.

Secondary infertility was turning out to be a particularly difficult thing to navigate through. I felt a lot of pressure to be thankful for what I had. I knew I was fortunate to have Aidan, and sometimes people would say to me, "What a blessing to at least have Aidan!"

I knew other women who were childless and would have traded spots with me in a heartbeat, thrilled to have just one child. I felt guilty for wanting more children, and yet in my heart, I didn't feel I should give up just because other women struggling with infertility would trade places with me.

All of these feelings stopped me from connecting with women who were going through primary infertility. I tried talking to my mom and my sister, but they hadn't walked in my shoes. One afternoon when I had just gotten my period, I felt like I was losing my mind. I sobbed and sobbed. Dirk had just walked in the door from work, so I tried to explain what I was feeling.

"I feel like a failure. I'm feeling so much pressure to give you five children. I keep picturing you on bended knee, asking me to have your five children."

Dirk shook his head in exasperation. "Well, that pressure is not coming from me. You're doing that to yourself."

This was not what I wanted to hear. I wanted him to take me in his arms and tell me that he loved me and that we would get through this together. I *did* want to have five children with him, and it wasn't fair to blame him for putting pressure on me. But yet, I felt it.

"We'll make an appointment with a specialist and figure it out," he said.

Dirk was a problem solver who always found the loophole through any challenge in business. I had always admired this about him, but today his words made me nervous. He had no idea how anxious I was.

When I gave Angela examples of my frustration, she pointed out that I needed affirmation, and Dirk didn't know how to give that to me. Expressing love to one another was no longer enough. We needed to find a way to understand one another.

There were days when we were fine. We would kiss before we left each other in the morning. Then I would go to counseling and have an epiphany that made me frustrated with him. When he came home that night and tried to kiss me, I was still processing, and sometimes wouldn't kiss him back.

I knew it was not necessarily fair to him. I was going through different emotions and excavating feelings of unworthiness I developed in my adolescence. I didn't see then that it was a self-fulfilling prophecy. I just saw myself as a failure.

Dirk had no idea all of this was going on inside of me. He was relying on the pattern of communication he had learned in his family, and in fairness, that same pattern had worked between us until now. He was doing the best he could to be supportive, but his words were not always reaching me.

I went to counseling every other Friday, and it took me a few days to process everything we discussed. The counseling sessions coincided with our weekly date nights and quite often, I found myself barely talking to Dirk. One night at dinner, he couldn't take the disconnection.

"Steph, you need to snap out of it and be present."

Dirk was right. This was the first serious crisis in our marriage, and I knew it would either bring us closer or drive us apart. Changing my counseling session to earlier in the week so we could enjoy a night out together was not a lot to ask. I wanted the counseling to improve our marriage, not destroy it. If nothing else, I knew that Dirk and I were committed to doing everything we could to make sure that what we were going through was just a season, and that we would come out on the other side even stronger.

CHAPTER 15

All Because of a Pink Lip Gloss

Throwing Stacy's shower was something I was really looking forward to but was also nervous about. I was friends with all of the shower guests, so I knew it would be a good time. The shower was an opportunity for us to get together and celebrate Stacy and her sweet baby.

Since it was Stacy's second child and she was having another girl, there wasn't much that she didn't already have. We had come up with a fun monogram theme for the gifts. While we all had a glass of champs at the shower, Stacy sipped her orange juice and opened her packages.

After Stacy and I packed up the car with all of the presents, we headed to a hospital supply rental company to run an important errand for Rennie. Just a few days before, he had torn his Achilles playing basketball. He was hobbling around and needed a scooter, so he asked us to pick one up for him on the way home. With the baby due in just a few weeks, Rennie's timing could not have been worse, and Stacy was not a happy camper.

"We should get him a pink scooter and tell him it was the only one they had," I suggested. We both laughed. I pointed out a turquoise scooter with a wicker basket on the front and she got a gleam in her eye.

"Oh, that's it," she said.

The thought of Rennie riding around the university campus where he worked and all over our small town on a scooter with a basket on the front made us laugh. By the time we packed it into the car with all of the baby gear we were laughing hysterically—almost crying. I wondered out loud as we drove along if Rennie would keep the scooter, since it was more fitting for someone's grandmother.

"Do you think he'll take it back?"

"I'm not taking it back." Stacy looked out the window and took a deep breath to suppress her laughter.

"Thank you for throwing me a shower. I know it was hard for you."

Stacy's words meant so much in that moment. It was her day and yet she was thinking about my feelings. I felt complete relief, and I also felt loved and supported. My emotions welled up as I looked over at her face.

"I'm so happy and so grateful that it worked out and you're not in my shoes," I said.

Stacy's brown eyes glistened with tears. "I'm serious—I would have a baby for you."

There seemed to be a pattern of people dropping big news on me when I was driving. Stacy's offer almost made me drive clear off of the highway. I hadn't ever thought about the notion of someone else carrying a baby for me. Stacy's gesture was powerful, and as unexpected as it was, it was in keeping with the way her mind worked. She was a problem-solving engineer. She had identified what seemed to be my problem—I could conceive children, but my body just couldn't seem to carry them.

Next to Dirk putting a ring on my finger and my giving birth to Aidan, Stacy's gesture was one of the most momentous occasions in my life. I was in awe of her generosity and love for me. Stacy was normally in control of her emotions, but they were getting the better of her.

"Oh my gosh, my hormones."

I thought back to the day all those years ago when I bought her the

MAC "Angel" lip gloss for her birthday. I cried and smiled at the same time.

"All of this because of a pink lip gloss."

Stacy cried some more. I didn't know that I would ever take her up on her offer, but her selflessness facilitated an even deeper level of friendship and sisterhood. I knew that she meant it. And I knew that if there was anyone on this earth that I would trust enough to carry my baby for me, it was she.

Little Miss Evie arrived that next month. I arrived at the hospital right after she was born. As I took her into my arms, I knew that the two of us would have a special bond. "Aunt Steph loves you!" I whispered to her as I looked into her big brown eyes.

CHAPTER 16

Hell's Bells

After a few months of counseling, Angela and I agreed that it was time for me to seek medical wisdom about my recurrent miscarriages. There seemed to be a pattern, and I needed to see a specialist to find out what was causing them. I was seeing Angela to help me process my feelings—but also to help me cope with worrying and devise a plan for my health.

I had *always* been a worrier. To a certain extent this was a trait I had inherited from my father, who was overprotective of us when we were growing up. He was obsessed with our safety. I still laugh hearing the story about when I was an infant—he wouldn't even let my mom lay me down on the floor beneath the living room chandelier for fear that in an earthquake I would be killed. As a teenager, he wouldn't let me try out for the pom squad, cheerleading or, for God's sake, even do the splits because of concern that I would hurt my hip.

My father's fears weren't completely irrational. I had been born with a congenital dislocation of the hip. To this day, it's a story my mother will share with anyone, even those she just met. When I was only four months old, my mother discovered that one of my legs was longer than the other. My pediatrician took one look at my hip and scooped me into his arms, running to the hospital next door. I was put into a body cast and was hospitalized for a month so that I could be in traction. I continued to wear a body cast for another nine months. My parents had to set me in a laundry basket just so I could sit up.

My rehabilitation went on until I was three years old. I transitioned to a half body cast and then a series of braces. Six months before I would finally be out of my last brace, I contracted double pneumonia on a road trip to Maine in our motor home and was rushed to the ER.

During my second hospitalization, my mom was able to maintain perspective. She knew there were children at the hospital who had illnesses far more serious than mine. My father did not rebound as easily. My hip dysplasia and pneumonia exacerbated his worries, so he always remained physically overprotective of me.

Unfortunately, I was in the same camp as my father. For years afterward, I needed reassurance that I was not sick. I have vivid memories of worrying about my health when I was a child. I would obsess about running a fever and followed my mom around the house asking her to take my temperature.

Thirty or so years later, it was time for another kind of temperature reading, but Angela's suggestion made me anxious. I had convinced myself that my recurrent miscarriages were because I had cancer, an autoimmune disorder, or some other rare and terminal disease. I could barely sit still on her couch as she looked at me with her unblinking eyes.

"Let's go through it. What if you *are* ill? Then what?"

Her question shocked me.

"I've got a child and a husband."

"What if you *did* die?"

Angela struck me as being out of line. I wanted her in my court. Instead, she was playing devil's advocate. She pointed out that Aidan would be fine. That he had Dirk and that Dirk could remarry and build another family for Aidan. The thought of that stirred up a fire and a feistiness in me.

"Hell's bells!" The one child that I had and he was going to be raised by someone else?

I always thought it was just my nature to be prepared for the worst, but I suddenly realized what Angela was doing. With every question she was holding up a mirror and reflecting my crippling fear back to me. I had lived with my obsessive thoughts for most of my life. It turned out I had a condition: *general anxiety disorder*. A light bulb went off in my head. I was dumbstruck as I stared at Angela.

"I'm thirty-eight and I'm just finding this out now?"

Suddenly, it all fell into place. The lasting impact of my childhood illnesses coupled with the instability of my adolescence. I began to laugh. I laughed and laughed and the tears started flowing. I was so relieved to have a name for it!

Until this very moment, I hadn't realized how powerful my fearful thoughts were. Sitting there on Angela's couch, I felt like I was looking at myself in the mirror and seeing myself for the first time. I was so thankful for the diagnosis, and overjoyed that it was something we could change and control. I started reflecting about how I would get a headache and would see someone on Dr. Oz's TV show who had brain cancer and convince myself that I did too.

Having a name for my anxiety made it a bit easier to call the specialist recommended by Dr. Allison. His next available appointment was not for two weeks, so naturally I was a mess. Waiting for my appointment and the inevitable battery of tests the doctor was sure to do caused me nothing but mental anguish.

Fortunately, I had plenty to keep me busy. I was still running our restaurant, volunteering, and of course, busy being a mommy and a wife. Still, I knew the only way I could get through the next two weeks was through prayer.

So many things had been thrown my way in the past few months and my thinking was so clouded that I was confused about my faith. I would never have turned my back on God, but he was definitely not giving me any answers. I felt like I was lost in the proverbial desert. It was hard to show up for God when he was not showing up for me in the way I wanted, but Dirk and I continued to go to church every Sunday.

There was a new couple coming to our Sunday school class. They were about ten years older than the rest of us and were looking for a new home church. From the very first moment class started, it was clear their views were different from everyone in our class. Their approach was somewhat "hail, fire, and brimstone."

Barbara, the wife, was a chemist at the university. She dressed plainly and wore no makeup or jewelry. It wasn't long before she pissed off and offended the ladies in our Sunday school class with some of her comments.

Having a big personality myself, I was empathetic to Barbara. After thinking about all the times my own opinions had been too big for my britches, I decided to email Barbara and invite her to our next class social. Barbara responded quickly to my email and was very frank in her belief that we needed to pray for the people in our class. The sentence definitely made me raise an eyebrow, but I didn't let her discourage me from putting out the welcome mat. There had been numerous times when I'd felt like I wasn't part of the life around me, and she reminded me of how it was to feel like an outsider.

Somehow our correspondence blossomed into a friendship. Despite her judgmental nature, Barbara was surprisingly open, so I wrote about my infertility and confessed that I was also having a faith crisis. She shared that she had recently given birth to her second son in her mid-forties with her current husband without any intervention from a fertility specialist. According to Barbara, she had just hunkered down and prayed. This was so unusual and unheard of that I of course wanted to know more.

She was the most unlikely of characters, but she was full of wisdom and strength, so I started to suspect that she might be a guardian angel. She worked just a mile from where I lived, so when she invited me to pray with her on her lunch hour, I said yes. "For where two or more gather, I am in their midst," she said.

Praying in the middle of a parking lot wasn't what most women in town did for lunch, but I knew Barbara had been sent to me to share her wisdom.

When I arrived, she had scriptures typed up. She slid into my car and we began. I had never prayed out loud, and I had never heard a woman lead a prayer. It was overwhelming. Barbara's voice was confident, and her words compassionate. As we sat there in my car, I could actually feel God's presence, and my anxiety started slipping away. After the hour was over, I felt lighter and calmer. I knew then God had sent Barbara— an unlikely angel—to guide me out of the desert of my faith crisis. She had brought with her the greatest gift—teaching me to pray. And I knew in my heart that this was how I would get through seeing the fertility specialist.

CHAPTER 17

The Deep Dark Sea

I had my typical anxious feelings on the morning I was scheduled to see the fertility specialist. I was sick to my stomach, and very quiet. Dirk held my hand as I looked out the car window. I was prayerful that I would find answers and find strength to overcome my worry and my anxiety.

The fertility specialist came highly recommended by Dr. Allison. He had helped countless families overcome their fertility issues. He was featured on daytime talk shows and had been written about in local newspapers, so I felt reassured that he was the one to give me hope.

The appointment was only a consultation—but I still felt emotionally vulnerable as a nurse led us down a hallway to an exam room. I couldn't take my eyes off of the large-scale collage of photographs of smiling moms and their newborns on the hallway wall. There was a similar shrine of newborns, most of them multiple births, on the wall of the exam room where the nurse matter-of-factly led me through a series of questions about my medical history.

After the intake was completed, she led us to the doctor's office. The walls behind his desk were lined with his numerous diplomas and impressive accolades. I had no idea what to expect from a consult with a doctor who specialized in fertility and endocrinology.

I couldn't help but feel like I was diving into the deep dark sea. The doctor breezed into his office. He was handsome, with slicked-back hair that gave him a distinguished and sophisticated air. His confidence filled the room. He took my hand, gave me a warm handshake, introduced himself, and then looked right at Dirk.

"What do you do for a living?"

Dirk was taken aback by the question. He was notoriously private about his various business ventures, and honestly it was a strange "go-to" question. Dirk responded with his usual discretion.

"I'm in long-term care."

"He's also an attorney." I spouted this off so the doctor would know to be a straight shooter with us.

We sat across from the doctor, and once again I was asked to go through my medical history. He listened with great care, made notes, and then looked up at me intently.

"I think I can help you, Stephanie. I will have to perform an exam, look at your ovaries and check your ovarian reserve. Then I'm going to do a procedure on your uterus. It's like a Roto-Rooter for your uterus. It's not a very glamorous term but there's very little pain, I assure you. It's very standard, and for three months it will increase your chances of getting pregnant."

A Roto-Rooter for my uterus? The expression certainly was not alluring and clearly wasn't a medical term, but I was game. I left the office feeling hopeful. The doctor seemed as knowledgeable and thorough as he was caring. I really liked him and believed he was the one who could make a miracle happen for us.

Dirk was more cautious and hesitant about the consultation as we headed down to the laboratory for blood work.

"Well, we'll see. I hope he can help us."

The next week I went back for my Roto-Rooter procedure. It was no surprise that when I checked in at the hospital, my usual "white coat syndrome" was flaring. I had Googled the procedure. It was designed to unblock fallopian tubes, and it was not the easy procedure the doctor had described.

My blood pressure was elevated and my heart was racing. On the day of the consultation I had to regroup when I saw them printing three sheets of blood-work stickers with my name on them. Somehow, I managed to survive the drawing of thirteen vials of blood. I was no stranger to having blood drawn.

It was awkward going to a male obstetrician. Up until now, I had only seen women. That fact alone was unnerving enough without the sight of the big X-ray machine hovering over me.

Today the doctor was suited up in his brilliant blue scrubs and his face was obscured by a mask. He was very businesslike as he sat down between my legs and inserted the catheter.

"Hi, Steph. Let's begin. You're going to some feel pressure. I am going to shoot the dye into your right ovary." I took a deep breath, preparing myself for that feeling of pressure. I had felt it before when I had ultrasounds, so I knew what to expect. Instead of pressure, I felt intense cramping. It was so painful I almost came off the table.

"Now I'm going to shoot the dye into your left ovary."

The sensation was so excruciating that I screamed. I reflexively bridged my hips and contracted my pelvis.

"Oh my God, that hurts!" I screamed.

"Please, lie back down."

I turned my head, searching on either side of me for something to grip on to. The doctor didn't have any comforting words for me. Only commands. "Please, lay flat. You're going to have to hold the dye." He instructed me to flip over on my side.

"Tilt. Lie back down."

The pain was worse than anything, even labor pains. The X-ray machine clicked away above me. It seemed like an eternity had passed before he asked me to turn over onto my other side, and then the torturous process began again.

As painful as the procedure was, I was mad as hell. Why didn't the doctor prepare me for this? I could only hope the procedure was as effective as he had promised.

When he was finished, the doctor pushed back and removed his gloves.

"Okay. You're done."

The doctor didn't help me get my legs out of the stirrups or sit up. In a matter of seconds, he was gone.

Three days later, one of his nurses called to tell me everything was normal. The doctor was putting me on a course of progesterone to prepare my body for conception and, more important in my case, help me maintain a future pregnancy. The nurse said they would call in a prescription and add to it after a week.

In no time at all, I had developed a spare tire about my abdomen. I was having terrible mood swings where I went from zero to a hundred, crying all the time. I was miserable to be around. My boobs looked like cantaloupes. Finally, I called the doctor's office and spoke to one of his nurses.

"I can't do this—the progesterone is making me crazy. Can we try something else? I am unbearable to be around."

The nurse sounded overworked and proceeded in a very matter-of-fact way.

"I will talk to the doctor, but he's going to say no. Suppositories are the only alternative."

Sex had become painful enough as it was. I couldn't imagine adding more discomfort into my day with a suppository. For the first time in our marriage, Dirk had no interest in being intimate. On my good days I was a bear, and on my bad days I reminded myself of Sigourney Weaver in *Ghostbusters*. Who wants to have sex with that? I finally decided to pull up my big-girl pants and make the best of it. It was only temporary, and I wanted to give us the best chance to have another baby.

Weeks later, I was looking at my calendar when I realized that I missed my period. I took a pregnancy test and it was positive. I stood there in my bathroom, in shock to think that somehow through all of this, I had managed to get pregnant in the first month.

CHAPTER 18

Scientific Proof

Early on in my appointments with Angela, she told me Dirk would have to come in with me. Apparently we had issues to work on as a couple. I knew that Dirk, like most men, would not be enthusiastic about this news. The night that I asked him to go to counseling with me, he didn't say yes right away. He was not used to communicating his feelings at all, let alone with a stranger. He needed time to process it. I knew he didn't feel like he needed help, but we had lost several pregnancies by now. This had brought us to the lowest point in our marriage.

I had a sour pit in my stomach the morning of the therapy session. As I stepped out of the shower, I got dressed while watching the *Today* show. Giuliana Rancic was being interviewed about going through IVF (in vitro fertilization) only to have her fertility specialist discover she had breast cancer. I had been a fan of hers and always watched her on the red carpet at the Academy Awards, Grammys, and on her reality show. Hearing her story made me realize that my situation could be worse.

Dirk and I had planned to attend a counseling appointment that afternoon. I wasn't worried he was going to leave me—I just wanted him to hear me out and validate my feelings.

At seven and a half weeks into my pregnancy we were cautiously optimistic, and shared the news with our families. I was exhausted and had the same food aversions that I did when I was pregnant with Aidan. I couldn't walk into the grocery store without almost vomiting at the smell of those rotisserie chickens.

I was so grateful for the fertility specialist. He was truly our saving grace. Our hands were sweating on the day he performed the ultrasound. I cried as we listened to our baby's heartbeat for the first time. It was nothing short of miraculous. We couldn't stop smiling at the image on the screen and the sound of our baby's heart beating inside me. The specialist was excited for us and very proud of his work.

"If you make it to nine weeks with two confirmation ultrasound heartbeats, you're good to go."

Hearing those words was like magic. We had less than two weeks to go until we reached that critical milestone, and then the worst would be behind us. I left his office and exhaled.

About a week later I woke up one morning to Aidan crying. I shot out of bed and ran to his room. As I rocked him, I realized that I did not feel pregnant. I wasn't tired or nauseous—and my body just felt *different* somehow. I immediately called the specialist's office and requested an appointment. His nurses always seemed overworked and were a bit too matter of fact for me. This time the nurse was downright short when she spoke to me.

"You were *just* here. You're due for another ultrasound next week. You'll need to wait."

"I'm telling you something is wrong. I want to be seen."

The nurse held her ground. "He's really busy today. You need to wait."

There was no way I was going to let an impatient nurse with a bad attitude make such an important decision. I insisted she put me on hold and consult with him. After being put on hold for a few minutes, the nurse returned to the phone. I could tell by the tone of her voice I had officially been labeled a pain in the ass.

"The doctor really feels like you should wait until next week, but he will squeeze you in this afternoon."

I was so nervous driving the forty miles up to his office. I knew in my heart that something was wrong. Or was it? Once I was in the examination room, my specialist strode in. He was very curt and let me know with his brusque manner that I was screwing up his schedule.

"Everything looks fine. There's a heartbeat. Okay? See you next week."

I couldn't help but feel a little foolish as I got dressed. Everything was normal. On the drive home I decided that it was time to hang up my worry and focus on being positive.

Two weeks later, it was graduation day for us. Once this appointment was over, we would not have to see a specialist anymore. I was really looking forward to returning to Dr. Allison for my prenatal care. I was feeling great as I lay down on the exam table in my thin cotton gown. The specialist turned on the ultrasound machine and placed the wand on my belly. He went quiet as he moved it around my little baby bump. Dirk grabbed my hand and squeezed it.

I was counting down the days in my head until we would find out the sex of our baby. I noticed in that moment that the doctor was pushing the wand around, staring intently at the screen. A full minute went by. His silence was unbearable.

His words were like a knife in my gut. "This is bad. This is very, very bad."

There was zero compassion in his voice. I remembered back to when Dr. Allison had to deliver the same news to me. She understood the depth of the devastation we were facing, and her voice was filled with empathy.

For the specialist, our loss seemed transactional. His own magic had failed him, and he didn't have any answers.

"This is very bad. There is no heartbeat. You'll need to go back down to the lab for blood work and I will see you here for a D&C in two days. You can set it up with the front desk."

Almost as an afterthought, he said "I'm sorry," as he walked out of the room. I think the apology was more to himself—we had reduced his success rate.

It felt like the wind had just been knocked out of us. We had come in confidently to hear our baby's heartbeat and left with surgical orders for a D&C. It was even more heartbreaking because the baby had prospered. We had heard the baby's heartbeat two times which, according to the specialist, was scientific proof that everything was okay—and yet it wasn't.

CHAPTER 19

The Messenger

The D&C was worse than the first time around. We had gone public with this baby, even sharing the news with our Sunday school class. Now my body had failed again, and I felt so guilty for bringing everyone along on this roller coaster ride with us. My mind was fearfully going to places it shouldn't have. I couldn't help but think about my sister, who was fourteen weeks pregnant with her first child. Thankfully she wasn't having issues.

Life was changing all around me. Gigi was living in a nursing home. My mother had a hip replacement and my father had a quadruple bypass. This was a wake-up call that my parents needed more support. We had talked them into moving to our town where we could be more supportive of them, and moved Gigi into the nursing home that Dirk and I owned.

After ten years, our church pastor was retiring. Our new pastor had been appointed by the district, and we had learned it was a woman. Knowing how difficult it was for women to get appointments, my mother-in-law commented that the new pastor had to be amazing in order to climb the rankings of the Methodist Church. It was evident that God was placing women in my life who were connected to Him.

One of the things Barbara had taught me to pray for was wisdom. Some people like to meditate and get answers through a quiet whisper, while others liked lightning bolts. I had learned that I needed messengers—angels, if you will.

I couldn't help but feel that our new female pastor was the shot in the arm I needed. When we met, the two of us immediately struck up a friendship. Pastor Linda was real, down to earth, and had the most peaceful energy. Her brilliant blue eyes made me feel like I could tell her anything. I told her about our fertility struggles within the first five minutes after we met. She took my hand, had tears in her eyes, and genuinely cared about our struggles. She was a mother, a woman, and she "got it."

I couldn't continue seeing a doctor who was missing a sensitivity chip, so I found a new female fertility specialist at the university medical center. Amongst other areas, she focused on recurrent miscarriages. Dr. Craig was in her third trimester on the day we met for our consultation. We were the same age, and she reminded me of one of my friends. She was very matter of fact, but was also empathetic and caring at the same time. A "tell it like it is" kind of gal if you will.

"Steph—I can treat you, but my success rates are better in women in a younger age range."

I appreciated how honest and straightforward she was with me. Truthfully, I didn't know what direction to go in or how to proceed. I still had the physical symptoms of my miscarriage going on, and I was in the midst of grieving.

It was hard to believe the end of the year had rolled around again. I had my hands full with work, volunteering, Christmas parties, and all of the other madness that comes with celebrating the holidays. One afternoon I was looking at my calendar and I realized—I had missed my period. Getting pregnant again was the farthest thing from my mind, so I hadn't kept track of my cycle. "Well, there's no way," I thought to myself.

After everything my body had been through just *two* months ago, I was doubtful I could be pregnant, but knowing how punctual my period was, I decided to take a pregnancy test. I shook my head as I watched the plus sign on the test come into focus. I couldn't believe it. I laughed out loud at the sweet surprise I had been given. The timing of it had God's fingerprints all over it. Dirk was in complete shock when I called him with the news of our Christmas miracle. I laughed and laughed. God had a sense of humor. It was happening on *his* time, not mine—I had decided.

Pastor Linda had given me her cell number, so I sent her a text asking her to call me. She called me back within the hour and I shared my crazy news.

"You'll never guess! I'm pregnant!"

Linda knew a little about what Dirk and I had been through, so our news was surprising to her.

"Congratulations! It's a Christmas miracle," she giggled.

It was a beautiful but scary moment for me. I knew I would have to rely on my faith to get me through the pregnancy, but in my heart I felt this was it. This was the one. This baby was going to make it. Not long after we got off the phone, Linda called me back.

"I don't know a whole lot about infertility . . . and this might sound a little weird, but I want to meet up with you so I can pray over you. I have a friend, Eve, who is one of the closest people to God that I know. With your permission, I would like to invite her to join us. Can you meet me in, let's say, an hour?" This was exactly what I needed to hear.

When I arrived, Linda and Eve were waiting for me in the church sanctuary. Eve was thin with short hair and a sweet smile. The lights from the Christmas garland twinkled and reflected light off of the hundred-year-old stained glass windows in the church. I was filled with emotion as I sat down on one of the wooden benches. Linda placed anointing oil on my wrists in the shape of the cross. It seemed like she had known me my whole life as she and Eve prayed for God to replenish and protect me. I had never heard women pray like this before. I felt so loved by these two women I hardly even knew.

My spirit was so moved that I spoke out loud the desires of my heart. I didn't know where it had come from, but I just went with it. I had never prayed in front of anyone before, except for Aidan. I trusted them so much in that moment and knew that God had sent these women to me. Warm, salty tears rolled down my chin onto my neck. They kept flowing and flowing. I was so overcome with emotion—fear, excitement—knowing that God was present.

I left the church feeling so hopeful. I could still feel the halo effect of Linda and Eve's prayers when Dr. Craig's office called to give me the blood test results. We estimated that I was five and a half weeks pregnant. Dr. Craig was out on maternity leave, so I scheduled my ultrasound with her partner, Dr. Hansen, for the following week.

The thought of having a doctor I had never met, a man no less, perform my vaginal ultrasound was not ideal, but I didn't have other options. Given the fact that I was high risk, Dirk and I were nervous about the ultrasound. The technician was dressed in bright blue scrubs, with her brown hair pulled back into a ponytail.

"Congratulations to both of you! How far along are you?"

She settled onto the stool and smiled at us as she turned on the machine.

It was quiet. I had grown to hate the quiet moments during ultrasounds. The technician squinted her eyes as she clicked buttons and took pictures.

"Hmmm. I'm not finding anything on the ultrasound. When was your last period? Your hCG test [which measures a hormone level detected in pregnancy] indicates you are pregnant, but I don't even see a sac. Let me look again."

Dirk and I sat in complete silence, holding hands while she gave it another look. Then came those familiar words.

"I am really sorry."

I wanted to vomit. I was so angry when she left the room. I couldn't believe this was happening again. I wanted to scream at God, "You sent me this pastor who prayed over my womb! At Christmas time too. Seriously?"

It was a terrifying moment when Dr. Hansen came into the room. He was tall, about my age, with dark hair and dark eyes. He was calm and kind. He introduced himself in a gentle voice.

"I am Dr. Craig's partner, Dr. Hansen. I promise you that you are in good hands. Now I know that we have never met before and this must be overwhelming for you. I want to perform another ultrasound and take a look to make sure we aren't missing anything."

He inserted the transvaginal ultrasound probe inside me. He looked at the screen and tilted his head to the right. He was extremely thorough in looking for our baby on the screen. Finally, he spoke.

"So, I am not seeing a gestational sac or a baby on the ultrasound. I am so sorry, Steph. It could be a chemical pregnancy, but what concerns me is that your hCG is so high. I would like to schedule a D&C. We will go in and explore and look for a fetus that might be in your ovary or your fallopian tube. We may not find anything, but it's best to be sure."

I was so confused. They couldn't see a baby inside me but they wanted to perform surgery on me?

Two days later I returned to Dr. Hansen's office for the procedure known as the "last look" ultrasound, which would give final confirmation that our baby did not have a heartbeat. It was a horrible procedure. I spent the morning praying for divine intervention. Maybe, just maybe, I wasn't as far along as we thought—and maybe the baby would appear on the ultrasound this time.

Dirk held my hand as Dr. Hansen turned on the machine, inserted the probe inside me, and moved it around. I couldn't bear to look at the monitor as the deep oceanic sounds of my womb filtered through the machine and into the room. Dr. Hansen stayed focused on the monitor.

"Oh—there's the heartbeat."

My heart raced as I heard my baby's heart beating from inside me. I looked over at Dirk, whose eyes were focused on the monitor. This was the miracle I had prayed for. My heart raced even faster. I couldn't help crying, but I couldn't understand why Dirk's face was so full of despair. I squeezed his hand. He looked at me with sad eyes and shook his head.

"It's in your fallopian tube."

Dr. Hansen nodded and measured his words carefully.

"It's a tubal pregnancy. It's not viable. I am so sorry."

Dr. Hansen explained that they would have to remove the baby from my fallopian tube and perform a tubal ligation.

Several days later, I went in for the procedure. I was so surprised when I saw Pastor Linda in the hospital lobby—waiting for us. It was completely unexpected. I gave her the hugest hug and squeezed her hand.

"Linda, I know that God sent you. Thank you for being an angel to me."

Her eyes were bright and peaceful, as always.

"Why don't we say a prayer?"

I nodded emphatically. There was nothing I would have liked more at this moment. We all held hands as Linda began the prayer.

"God, we don't know why this is happening and we're sad for Stephanie and Dirk. Please place her in the palm of Your hand and give her peace. You know her heart's desire. Please guide the surgeon's hands and take Steph in your care."

In that moment I was so grateful for Linda. She was a bright light at the end of a dark tunnel. I felt comforted by her presence, yet I was so full of dread and despair too. She was an angel sent to comfort me and represent God. I was sad and bewildered, but I knew deep down there was an underlying message from God.

"I can't change what happened, but I am here. I've got you."

CHAPTER 20

Practicing Medicine

I woke up in the recovery room a good two hours after the procedure, surrounded by Dirk, my mom, and Pastor Linda. I was on such powerful drugs that I was not capable of anything beyond facial recognition. This was my third surgery to have one of our babies removed from my body. Because this was an ectopic pregnancy, Dr. Hansen had performed the tubal ligation by laparoscopy. It was the latest technology, and it allowed them to go in through my belly button and make small incisions in the corners of my abdomen instead of making a larger incision.

Even though it was a medical advancement, it still felt very different from a D&C. I had so much pain from having my fallopian tube cut. Despite being heavily drugged, there was no question that I had undergone surgery.

It was midafternoon by the time I got home. I could not have been any happier to see our bed. I was drugged completely out of my mind, so Dirk and my mom helped me up into the bed and carefully tucked me in. Beneath the waistband of the sweatpants I was wearing, I could see the gauze on my belly button from where Dr. Hansen had made the incision.

Had I been in a clearer state, I might have even been annoyed with Dirk for running out to a business meeting in the city as soon as he tucked me in. All I could think about was going to sleep. Thankfully, Aidan was with my mom just at the other end of the house in the event that I needed anything.

It was raining cats and dogs when I woke up about three hours later. I felt so bloated and heavy that even the slightest movement was excruciating. I needed to go to the bathroom but I knew there was no way I could get up on my own, so I called to my mom.

With the rainstorm pounding on the roof my voice must not have carried down there, because thirty minutes later I was still yelling to her for help.

My need to use the bathroom was urgent, so despite the pain I was in, I swung my legs off the side of the bed. They were like gelatin beneath me. I collapsed onto the hard floor. The last thing I heard before I passed out was the sound of my head hitting that floor.

The rain was still pounding on the roof when I came to about a half hour later. I was delirious by now. I couldn't help laughing as I called for my mom, one more time.

"What the hell? So much for helping me."

I was determined to get to the bathroom, so I army-crawled— dragging my heavy legs behind me. I knew I must have been such a sight. It was no easy feat pulling myself up onto the toilet with the dead weight of my legs beneath me, but somehow I managed. I was completely exhausted by the time I got myself up into a seated position. I bore down and felt a "pop" from my belly button.

I looked down and saw an enormous gush of blood emerge from behind the gauze on my belly button. My wound gurgled as blood and fluid flowed from my incision. It was so terrifying, it completely woke me from my haze. Within a minute, the blood had soaked my sweatpants, run down the toilet and my legs onto the floor, and saturated the bathroom rug.

I used my fingers to plug my belly button and slow the flow of the blood. The gurgling was absolutely the most horrific sound I had ever heard. I screamed hysterically for my mother. I didn't know if she had heard me or if she just happened to check on me, but I was so relieved to hear her voice in the bedroom.

"I'm the bathroom!"

When the bathroom door swung open and my mom stepped through it, I thought she was going to pass out.

"Oh my God."

I knew I needed to lie down.

"Can you help me? I need to lie flat."

Somehow my mom managed to stay calm as she helped me onto the floor. She grabbed one of our oversized white Pottery Barn bath towels, and then a second one. She used them to apply pressure on the incision to stop the bleeding. I obviously needed an ambulance, but I wanted to get in touch with Dirk first to let him know what was happening.

My mom handed me my phone and I sent him a text: *Call me ASAP. It's urgent.* When there was not an immediate text from Dirk, my mom called him a couple of times and left him voicemails. In between, we kept applying pressure to the incision. Finally, Dirk called my mom. I could tell she was trying not to scare me as she spoke to Dirk.

"Steph is lying here on the floor of the bathroom. She's bleeding from her belly button. We've been putting pressure on it to stop it, but every time we stop, it starts again. She's lost a lot of blood and needs an ambulance."

In situations like these, Dirk was always very calm and clear minded. Today was no different. As soon as he hung up with my mom he was going to call Dr. Hansen. I had been through one C-section and three D&Cs, and I knew my body. I didn't think I was dying, but I knew I needed medical attention. Being in the elder-care business, Dirk spent his days surrounded by doctors and the nursing home residents recovering from surgeries, and was experienced in handling medical emergencies. I understood his wanting to size up the situation himself.

By the time he arrived, our bathroom looked like a murder scene. His reaction was the opposite of most people; he was calm and methodical. He had already spoken with Dr. Hansen and knew that it was probably peritoneal fluid and blood coming from my incision. I was still frightened and wanted to call an ambulance, but Dirk's instincts were different.

"Steph, trust me. Just let me take you to the hospital."

It was still pouring outside. We wrapped two beach towels around my abdomen and Dirk held an umbrella over me as we made the short walk to the car. I reclined the seat as we drove to the closest emergency room. When we arrived, Dirk ran inside and grabbed a wheelchair for me. Once we were inside, the emergency room staff wheeled me onto a gurney and took me straight into the triage area.

My blood loss was obvious to the emergency room doctor, who was a twenty-something lady with jet black hair and little brown eyes. She was reluctant to touch my open wound, since my specialist was affiliated with a different hospital. Because my surgery had taken place more than twelve hours prior, I was a huge risk to her. She was communicating with Dr. Hansen and ordered lab work to make sure I was stable and to assess my blood loss. I was also dehydrated, so they started me on an IV drip.

"We're going to keep you here until the bleeding stops."

While I lay there on the table, I remembered Dr. Hansen explaining he would be using Dermabond, a surgical glue, on the belly button incision he had made. According to the emergency room doctor, when I bore down to go to the bathroom, the glue in my belly button "popped" because of the pressure. I laughed. Of course! My luck.

It took about two hours for the bleeding to wind down to a trickle. We were starting dismissal paperwork with a nurse, but my relief was short lived. Out of nowhere I felt shoulder pain so excruciating, I thought I was going to die. I screamed and gripped the sides of the hospital bed.

"Oh my God, Dirk! You have to help me. I can't take this pain! What is going on? Oh-My-God! Please help me!"

Pain radiated from my breasts up my collarbone and into my shoulders. It was so sharp, so severe, that I couldn't help but scream bloody murder. Dirk looked down at my face and ran to get the nurse.

The doctor assessed me quickly and ordered pain meds, *stat*. She explained that the CO_2 Dr. Hansen had injected into my abdomen to give him a better view of my fallopian tube during the surgery had irritated my nerves and was causing the pain. It was known as deferred shoulder pain and was very common after this kind of surgery. I couldn't believe this was happening. I thought I had bottomed out medically with the bleeding, but it turned out there was a new low.

I was shocked that they were hooking me up to a morphine drip, but so grateful for it at the same time. As the pain began to subside, I felt exhausted physically, mentally, and emotionally. In that moment, I completely surrendered myself to God and asked Him to take care of me.

"I'm all yours. Please God, help me."

One week later, when I finally went in to see Dr. Hansen for my follow-up appointment, I could tell he genuinely felt horrible. We all make mistakes, and I could see he was remorseful. I appreciated his apology. He was a doctor and a specialist, but he was still human. He assured me that he would not use the Dermabond on another patient. Unlike God's, his knowledge was limited, and I learned that's why they call it *practicing* medicine.

CHAPTER 21

Sum'r Teeth

Aidan's fourth birthday came around just after the New Year. He had lost interest in John Deere and had become obsessed with a reality television show on Animal Planet called *Call of the Wildman*. The show was about a Kentucky woodsman nicknamed "Turtleman" who had a unique talent for capturing every critter known to man—from giant snapping turtles to skunks—with his bare hands. Turtleman had what I called "Sum'r Teeth," meaning that *sum r there and sum r not*. Aidan didn't seem to notice, and chose Turtleman as the theme for his birthday party.

Planning the party was a welcome change from everything that Dirk and I were going through. We booked a party space at the local natural history museum, and I even found Turtleman shirts online. Our whole family dressed in camo for the party, including my in-laws and my parents. There I was—a total city slicker sporting a camo cowboy hat, camo pants, and a Turtleman T-shirt. Not everybody knew who Turtleman was, so a few of the guests at the party and visitors to the museum thought we had absolutely lost our minds. The things we do for our kids!

Most guests wouldn't have known that it was a dark time for me. I seemed to make progress between miscarriages, but then it was one step forward and two steps back. After this last tubal pregnancy, my head was spinning. I had gone from pregnancies to losing a baby at close to the end of my first trimester and now an embryo inexplicably lost in my fallopian tube.

Once again I was wracked with feelings of grief, guilt, and unworthiness. My grief and sadness had expanded inside me. It was all that I felt. I went through periods when Angela guided me through my feelings. "This is not your fault," she said at my appointment after the D&C for my tubal pregnancy.

She encouraged me to grieve in concrete ways. I kept a box of memories of our babies—the positive pregnancy tests, notes and letters from friends, medical paperwork, photos from ultrasounds. Each year the content in the box would grow and grow. It did help to have tangible items to help me remember the babies that we lost.

Angela also helped me come up with a plan to center myself. She helped to shift my frame of mind into acceptance. This didn't mean that I had to accept that I was infertile, but I did have to accept that I had a challenge, a condition. I had to acknowledge this and approach it with hope instead of fear. She encouraged me to give my worries to God and to communicate with Him more often.

Aidan was conscious of being an only child. He wanted a sibling, and every night when we tucked him into bed and said his prayers with him, he asked God to send him a little brother or sister. We had sheltered Aidan from my health issues. He knew mommy had doctor's appointments and got sick but we kept everything normal for Aidan so he would never be frightened or confused.

Despite my recurrent miscarriages, I didn't try to persuade Aidan's prayers otherwise. Although I didn't know what would happen, it was his petition to God and I trusted that God was listening to him.

CHAPTER 22

Flood Plain

At this point, my health, our family, and the future were all unclear. There were no answers anywhere, and everything in our lives seemed to be on hold. Even the lot Dirk and I had purchased for our future family home was still sitting empty.

Although we hired an architect and he had drawn up plans, we were apprehensive about moving forward because we didn't know what our family would look like. If it would be just the three of us, we didn't need more than a couple of bedrooms. If we were going to have more children, we'd need a bigger house because we wanted them to have their own bedrooms. And we were afraid that if we moved forward on the plans without confirmation of how many children we were going to have, we might jinx things.

We also had a small group of neighbors that were contesting our trying to build on a lot that was partially in the flood plain. They were very determined to stop us, and even put up a website that said *O'Haras, Don't Flood Our Homes.* I had always gotten along with my neighbors, so this was really hard for me—so much so that it sent my heart into a state of tachycardia. I had no idea what that was, but for three entire days, I experienced a heart rhythm disorder and had a full-blown panic attack. I wasn't able to sleep, control or slow my heart rate, or think about anything else until four days later.

Ironically, the lot that was supposed to represent our future had become a symbol of the barrenness that I felt inside. Dr. Craig had returned from her maternity leave, so I went in for my second appointment. She suggested genetic testing to us, because of my age. I wanted to know if there was something wrong with me or if there was something abnormal chromosomally with my babies. Dr. Craig explained that performing this kind of advanced testing was a bit out of her scope. The two of us had great rapport. As always, Dr. Craig was very direct, which I loved. I asked her if she were me, what would she do?

"If I were you, I would go see Dr. Schoolcraft in Denver. He's the best in the world. I am better at treating women who are younger than you. He has better success rates with women your age. Although I can do genetic testing on embryos at three days old, he can test them at five days old, when they have double the amount of cells."

Dr. Craig explained that Dr. Schoolcraft had helped couples who had failed elsewhere using IVF. I was overwhelmed by the idea of traveling all the way to Denver, not to mention leaving Aidan for an extended period of time. Honestly, I also didn't know if I agreed with the principles behind IVF. I needed to do some research and learn more about it.

I was undecided on my path and couldn't imagine what was next. Some days I found myself walking on our lot, where I would reflect and pray for wisdom. Other days I prayed with two dear girlfriends from Sunday school, Val and Melanie, who were also experiencing similar secondary fertility issues. We opened our hearts and prayed together in the chapel.

I was hesitant to get pregnant again unless I was being guided by a specialist. Since the genetic testing wasn't an option for now, Dirk and I agreed to avoid getting pregnant. I was absolutely terrified and worried about getting pregnant. After all, my issue wasn't conceiving; it was keeping the pregnancy. Each time I would see the positive test, it would prove to be more dangerous than the last pregnancy. We were having somewhat of a sexless summer, and it had taken all the romance and spontaneity out of our marriage.

It was helpful that Dirk and I were seeing Angela together. I knew that Dirk didn't necessarily care for Angela. I also knew firsthand that going to counseling didn't always feel good at first. The feelings that were unearthed in these sessions were powerful and resonant, so the fact that Dirk was committed to our appointments made me feel optimistic.

We had come to understand one another on a deeper level. Angela had us read the book *Five Languages of Love*, and we had learned a lot about one another and ourselves. Dirk needed what was called Acts of Service, which means doing something for your spouse that you know they would like for you to do.

There were many other small things that I found out he liked and didn't like. This little book turned out to help us learn to love each other the way we wanted to be loved.

I, on the other hand, needed to hear words of affirmation, which included Dirk absolving me of blame for our inability to have more children. He had never placed blame on me, but he had also never said it wasn't my fault. He had no way of knowing how deep rooted my feelings of failure were. His response was the same as always.

"You're putting the pressure on yourself, honey."

Angela, who always listened attentively, jumped in. "Okay, but you guys need to stand toe-to-toe. You are not acknowledging her feelings. She needs you to say, 'I love you regardless. Let's go through this together. Let's hold hands.'"

As awkward as it was, Dirk and I held hands and looked into one another's eyes. He told me that he loved me, that he didn't blame me and wasn't upset with me. He added that no matter what our family looked like—if it were just the three of us or if there were more babies to come—he felt blessed. He told me that I was punishing myself for something that wasn't my fault, and it was time to let it go. He missed his happy-go-lucky wife. Tears flowed down my cheeks and spilled down my neck. Hearing these words truly lifted a weight off of me. He was right. It was time to stop being so hard on myself and turn it over to God.

When we walked into our appointment that day, we were definitely in the trenches with no relief on the horizon. We still couldn't break ground on our lot or move forward on expanding our family, but we had managed to stop the emotional headstream, which had reached its high mark, from overtaking the flood plain of our marriage.

CHAPTER 23

The Paradox

My sister was still nursing Tripp, my newborn nephew, so she wasn't able to come visit me before or after my last surgery. When she called one night to check in on me, I was having one of those moments when I was really mad at God. Mel's hormones were still raging, so she was emotional too. We were quite the pair. Mel was also full of questions.

"How much more can you take? How much more can God let you encounter?"

The confusion, sadness, and frustration in her voice mirrored how I was feeling inside. It made me stop and think about everything that had happened over the last four years. Mentally and emotionally I had been through more than I ever thought I could bear. My body had also been put through so much.

I felt betrayed by God in a way. It was a strange feeling, but I knew he could handle my anger. Here he had sent Linda to me. She had prayed over me, yet somehow this horrible loss had happened again. It was awful, and I found myself asking God for answers. It was in the early mornings and at night when the house was still that I heard myself asking the same question over and over again.

"Why, God? Why?"

As disappointed as I was, I still trusted that I was not supposed to give up on having more children. I also wasn't throwing out my faith. It was a true paradox. As hopeless and heartbroken as I was, I felt God's presence. Praying brought me so much peace, and all around me I could see the people God had sent to help me.

My marriage was in a deeper place and somehow my struggles had made me become more confident.

Dr. Craig had recommended this specialist in Colorado. The thought of traveling out of state for up to a month for fertility treatments sounded so daunting and terrifying. Could I muster the strength to do this again? I decided I would pray and ask God to send me a sign.

CHAPTER 24

The Burning Bush

The next morning, I woke up early as usual to get Aidan ready for kindergarten. I felt like I had a mountain to climb, so I asked God for guidance. Our morning routine was virtually the same as it had been since he was a toddler. These last four years, I always made sure we had our "special cuddle time" in my bed. Except now, instead of quietly drinking his bottle while I sipped my coffee, Aidan played while I watched the *Today* show.

Even though it had only been a few minutes since I had prayed and begged God to send me a sign to direct me in my decision making, I was absolutely stunned when I turned on the television and saw Giuliana Rancic again. She was back on *Today*, doing a follow-up story on infertility and breast health. She shared details about her cancer treatment and the procedure she had done to save her eggs. Because of the drugs she was taking postcancer, she and her husband, Bill, had used IVF to have their embryo transferred to a gestational carrier. I sat there in my bed listening to Giuliana praise her fertility specialist.

"The fertility clinic we used in Colorado, Dr. Schoolcraft, referred us to an agency for gestational carriers."

I sat straight up. This was way too crazy, even for me. Here was Giuliana Rancic talking about the very same doctor recommended to me by Dr. Craig. I don't believe in coincidences, but what was happening was too much for me to process. My heart started racing and the hairs on my arms stood straight up. I was in complete shock!

After the interview I got Aidan ready for school and tried to go about the rest of my day. I couldn't stop thinking about what had happened. Who knew that God would speak to someone through the *Today* show?

That night at dinner I told Dirk about what had happened that morning. We were very different when it came to communicating with God. For Dirk, it was a voice in his head that guided him. For me, God always knew that I needed a sign or a messenger in human form. The timing of my seeing Giuliana Rancic on television talking about Dr. Schoolcraft was very interesting to Dirk. He agreed it very well might be the sign I was looking for.

I felt like I was standing at a fork in the road and didn't know which path to step onto. My questions weren't of a spiritual nature. I had already met with Pastor Linda, and she was supportive of IVF. She believed that God had invented science and technology and had made it available to us to grow his kingdom.

As usual, I was already thinking six steps ahead—anticipating the hormones and other drugs I would have to put into my body without any promise of a healthy, full-term pregnancy. The progesterone had turned me into a lunatic before, so that was not something I was looking forward to revisiting. There was also the excruciating Roto-Rooter procedure I had already undergone and would likely have to repeat. I didn't know if I could submit myself to that kind of unbearable physical pain again.

The worst part for me was the burden on my family. I was well aware that it wasn't just me and Dirk on this journey. We had the feelings of our families to consider. After my last miscarriage, my mother-in-law had tearfully said, "I just don't know how much more of this we can take." In all of these years I had only seen her cry once, so I knew her pain was profound. I felt guilty for having taken her on this roller coaster with us.

Then of course there was the reality that I would have to leave Aidan for weeks at a time if we went to Colorado. The thought of that made me sad. I knew he would be in the best possible hands with my parents and my in-laws, but the thought of him missing his mommy and daddy was unbearable to me.

Even though I wasn't one hundred percent convinced, I decided to check out Dr. Schoolcraft's website. I felt like Dorothy in *The Wizard of Oz* as I scrolled through the pages and clicked on tab after tab. This was a whole new world of medicine with dimensions I could not have imagined. I was completely overwhelmed by all of the information on everything from managing expectations to genetic testing and their rigorous medical protocol. It was an incredible amount of information to absorb. I poured myself a glass of wine as I spent the next two hours on their site.

The next morning I woke up and thought, "You know what? It doesn't hurt to make an appointment for a phone consultation." I didn't have to commit to flying out to Colorado, and the phone call would allow me to see if I even liked the doctor.

Once I had gotten Aidan off to school, I took a deep breath and dialed Dr. Schoolcraft's number.

My heart was racing and my hands were clammy as I was transferred from the receptionist to the scheduler.

"Yes, we can get you a phone consult. However, he was just mentioned on the *Today* show, so his next available appointment isn't until August."

I could have just kicked myself. The doctor's appointment was months away. Here I had summoned God and asked for a sign and He had responded almost immediately. I had gotten the nudge that morning on television—but I didn't listen.

It wasn't that I had chosen to ignore the sign God had sent me. The truth was that I was scared, and my fear had clouded my ability to act. Like Giuliana Rancic, I would have to undergo extensive testing including a mammogram as part of Dr. Schoolcraft's protocol. I was worried I might have an autoimmune disorder or worse, cancer. Up until now, none of the specialists I had seen had been able to diagnose my condition, so there was no indication of what it might be.

We essentially had an entire summer before our scheduled phone consultation. The lengthy window was both a blessing and a curse. Practically speaking, it gave me time to research the medical side of things. It also brought me a presence of mind that made me live every single day in a more intentional way.

I hadn't done a show with my band in three years, so I decided to book a gig for us. Being a Libra, I liked having a balance of my "regular" life—being a mom, wife, and business owner—with my creative side. Being on stage is my happy place. I love singing to people and making them forget their worries for a couple of hours. For me, performing with my band filled my cup. I would ride on an emotional high for weeks after being on stage. I missed it and was excited to get back into it.

The show was amazing. We played to a packed house of hundreds of people. Of course, there was Melissa in the front row, with her party hat on, and Stacy was dancing right beside her.

Even though Dirk and I were enduring yet another somewhat sexless summer, we made the best of it. In June, it was harvest time at the family farm so we spent a lot of time there. We also took Aidan on short road trips to the beach in South Texas and to Branson, Missouri. It was so relaxing to spend time with my little family and not think or worry about anything else.

As mindful and present as I was, this time felt like the calm before the storm. There was a decision looming on the horizon, and it was mine to make. I couldn't escape the feeling of pressure from myself. I knew now it wasn't Dirk. The weight I felt on my shoulders came from my own desire to give Aidan a sibling and to get answers about what was wrong with my body.

When the morning of the phone consultation finally came, I

returned home from dropping Aidan at school and prayed for wisdom. I had a daily prayer ritual that included a sweet pocket cross Pastor Linda had given me. It was made from wood from the holy land. I loved having something tangible to hold on to while I prayed. I would settle into my bedroom and recite James 1:5—"If you ask God for wisdom, he will give it in abundance."

I prayed that if seeking treatment for my infertility from Dr. Schoolcraft was meant to be, then I would see that. I asked God to make it clear to me.

Since Dirk was at the office, we set up a three-way call with the doctor. All these months I had built him up in my mind, so I was surprised that he was soft spoken and his comments very brief. He was well versed in my history, and there was no sales pitch.

"I'm confident you have a sixty-five percent chance to have a baby."

As he spoke, I suddenly felt like I had been holding my breath for six months and could finally exhale. I could tell Dirk did too as the doctor continued, "We'll do an initial one-day workup on you, which will consist of all sorts of tests. Then, if we undergo IVF, we will do genetic testing and ICSI [an IVF technique in which a sperm cell is introduced into an egg cell through medical intervention]. Your protocol will be based on what I find."

I wasn't sure if I was on board, but I heard myself say, "Okay, let's do this."

Their next availability for the one-day workup was over a month away, at the beginning of October. As I listened to myself schedule the appointment, I knew in my heart I might not keep it. The doctor was world renowned, but there was still no promise of anything. Yet whatever decision I made, it would change the trajectory of our little family.

For the next month I felt like that spider frantically spinning its web again. I didn't know what direction to go in. I had all of these confusing feelings in my head that filled me with worry. I knew the best thing I could do was dig deep in the trenches of prayer. I spent the next two weeks praying on my knees.

"I don't know what to do. I need a bigger sign. I need for you to send me a burning bush to show me the way."

Some nights when I was sleepless, I would roll over in the middle of the night and simply pray, "Help me." I knew that God spoke in clarity and I knew that he understood my need for a major sign. If I didn't get one, I wasn't going to make a move.

One night after putting Aidan to sleep, I climbed in bed with Dirk. He was reading our local paper. He crinkled the paper down so I could see one of the articles.

"Here's a piece I think you'll want to read."

It was an article on none other than Giuliana Rancic. She was coming to town to speak at the university on Friday. My arm hairs stood up. I looked up at the ceiling and said, "Okay, I'm listening." The fact that she was coming to our little college town was noteworthy. God definitely had my attention.

The next morning I woke up to a text from my friend Kate, who worked at the university. *Do your parents still have a limousine company? I have a celebrity airport transfer I need to schedule.* "Whoa," I thought. My arm hairs stood up again. I quickly texted her back: *Yes! And by the way, I know who you're talking about. Here's my parents' number.*

There was no question God had heard me and had sent me a sweet sign. I was tuned in now to what was happening. I didn't know Kate well, but I felt compelled to call her and let her know what was going on.

"This is going to sound really kooky and weird. I'm scheduled to see her doctor next week, but I'm scared. I've been praying for a sign to tell me whether I should go or not. I've been thinking about canceling my appointment."

Kate didn't miss a beat. "Why don't you come to the event?"

I had already committed to an event at a museum on Friday night, so I couldn't attend the forum. Kate suggested that I attend the reception *beforehand*, which was exactly the solution I needed.

When Friday finally came around, I felt like a child on Christmas morning. I walked into the reception, which was filled with chattering college girls. I was immediately handed a waiver, since Giuliana Rancic was filming for her reality show, "Giuliana and Bill."

After a couple of minutes, Kate strode into the reception from one of the back rooms and came straight over to me with an excited look on her face.

"Giuliana wants to meet you. I hope you don't mind, but I told her all about you."

It was all happening so fast, I didn't have time to think about how I felt. Kate escorted me into another room, and there in the corner was Giuliana Rancic, surrounded by her cameramen and their lights. Kate yelled across the room. "Giuliana, this is my friend, Steph." Giuliana wasted no time whipping around and walking straight toward me with her camera crew in tow. She grabbed both of my hands and jumped right in.

"Steph, Kate told me your story. You have to go to Colorado. You have to keep your appointment next week. Dr. Schoolcraft saved my life and gave me my little boy. He is going to do the same thing for you that he did for me!" she said.

I was so filled with emotion that I burst into tears. I was doing the ugly cry when I realized the film crew was capturing our intimate moment. There I was, a total hot mess, and I knew that this moment was going to be aired on her reality show. I couldn't help but laugh at was happening. Somehow I managed to regain my composure and shift my focus back to Giuliana. I told her how worried I was about having a mammogram. She looked at me with her reassuring brown eyes.

"Your mammogram is going to be fine. When this event is over, I'm going to text Dr. Schoolcraft and tell him you're my friend. This is your sign."

We chatted a good five minutes—just as two women who were warriors of infertility. We "got" each other. Before I left, Giuliana and I took a picture together. I knew my mom would never forgive me if I didn't get a picture with her for the scrapbook.

"Holy shit" was the only thought I could compose when I got back to my car. As overcome as I was, I didn't want to leave without acknowledging to Giuliana that I knew God had used her as an instrument. I ran across the street to a little gift shop and found an ornament that was a pair of angel wings. It was the perfect gift. I also got her a card and wrote a note: *Thank you for being my angel and for being my sign.* I gave it to her chauffeur and thanked him for passing it on to her.

I was stunned and shocked for the rest of the night. I marveled that for the better part of a year, God had been weaving this tapestry for me. I didn't know it until the moment I was face-to-face with Giuliana, but it had been God's plan for me all along. This whole time, he had been listening to me. He also knew me so well that when I asked for a burning bush, he knew he had to deliver big-time.

CHAPTER 25

The Trek

It was October and the Denver airport was full of travelers who were sporting climbing gear and sunburned faces. Their excitement and super-relaxed vibe was palpable, and mirrored my own free spirit. God had given me my sign and for the first time in years, I was free of the heavy worry. I had a new confidence, mental strength, and trust.

All around us we could see the gorgeous Rocky Mountains. As we drove along, I thought about how they symbolized the mountain we were trekking up as a family. Dr. Schoolcraft's clinic, the Colorado Center for Reproductive Medicine (CCRM), was just over an hour outside of Denver. My one-day workup wasn't until the next day, but Dirk and I were both such nerds, we decided to go ahead and check out the building.

It was dusk when we arrived, so the parking lot was empty. I could see the outline of the monumental building against the evening sky. It was very impressive. It was a hospital, surgery center, and lab all in one. Dirk and I knew right then and there we were exactly where we were supposed to be. There was no question that Dr. Schoolcraft's approach would take us to the next stage of our climb.

The next morning we were up before the roosters for our early start at the clinic. Dirk had a small breakfast while I drank my coffee, and then we prayed together. We thanked God for lining up our pathways with Dr. Schoolcraft and for opening this door for us. We also asked for His favor expanding our family. Dirk and I had done everything we could, mentally and physically, to give ourselves the best possible chance of success, but we knew that ultimately it was in the hands of God.

It wasn't quite seven in the morning, but the parking lot was already full of cars. We immediately noticed that the majority of them were rentals. I felt comfort knowing that a lot of the other patients had traveled a long distance to see Dr. Schoolcraft, just like us.

I had a gulp in my throat as Dirk and I walked into the clinic and checked in. In the middle of the lobby was a soothing waterfall. Over the years I had become accustomed to my "white coat syndrome" being soothed by talk shows and HGTV blaring from a flat screen television in the waiting rooms. The peaceful, soft, and calming sounds of the waterfall in the lobby created a very cool atmosphere that kept my thoughts in the present.

I was introduced to my nurse, Katie. She was a Midwestern gal and was very encouraging, sweet, and organized. She would be my nurse for the entirety of my treatment at CCRM. She handed me my schedule, which was daunting. We were booked through until the end of the day. Even Dirk had a schedule for the day. I could tell he was surprised.

"Whoa, I've got appointments too."

He paled a bit at the section in the timetable during which he was scheduled to give a semen sample. For years I had been the one to go through everything. I had been poked and prodded, many times with him in the room. It was time for comic relief. I winked at the nurse.

"I'm totally going in there with you when you give that semen sample!"

"No, you're not."

"Oh, yes I am. It's only fair. How many times have you been in the room when they're poking and prodding me?"

"That's different. You don't have to perform. You're not coming in, honey."

Katie and I had a good laugh. Fortunately for Dirk, I had a test that overlapped with his big moment.

Our first appointment of the morning was a class on in vitro fertilization. The nurse who was leading the class gave us a binder full of material that was two inches thick. As I leafed through it, I saw how comprehensive the information was—everything from medical jargon to legal documents determining ownership of the embryos. It was hard to believe the nurse was going to try to cover all of it in just sixty minutes.

We were one of a dozen couples from all over the country: Illinois, Massachusetts, California—even Canada and China. It was incredible to be in a room with all of these couples who had gone through what we had gone through. As hard as it was to believe, some of them had been through worse. Others had never even been able to conceive at all. We immediately felt an unspoken connection with our classmates and felt like we were all warriors together.

It was right after the first class that our tests began. Once again, I had to submit myself for the "Roto-Rooter" procedure. It had been looming ahead all of these months and I was absolutely dreading it. It was such an excruciatingly painful test that the thought of doing it a second time gave me serious pause.

Today it would be a nurse who administered the test. She was older, probably in her late fifties. I expressed my concern and anxiety about the pain I was about to endure during the procedure. She was calm, confident, and reassuring at the same time.

"Honey, I hear that all the time. We have a machine that is state of the art. I promise you, you're not going to feel a thing and it will be over in less than five minutes."

I was doubtful about her reassurance as I placed my legs in the stirrups. I was in disbelief when the whole procedure was done in five minutes, just as she had said. It made me so angry to know that the specialist who had performed the procedure back home was using antiquated machinery.

My next appointment was a routine gynecological exam with Dr. Schoolcraft, followed by a couples counseling session. The counselor was around the age of my mother. She had gray hair, round glasses, and a sweet smile. I was comfortable in her presence.

Unlike our sessions with Angela, where we focused on working through issues in our marriage, this counseling session made us feel understood. The counselor had met with thousands of couples and had heard it all. She spoke the same lingo that we did and understood the emotional and mental duress we had experienced. Even though she was a stranger, we had an unspoken trust with her.

We discussed all of the decisions that we would have to make, including how many embryos to transfer and other legal concerns. We also talked about Aidan and the effect that our absence might have on him while we were in Colorado. She then talked about the emotional support that I would need from Dirk during the medical protocol of shots.

At five o'clock we exhaled. We had completed our rigorous day and headed to the airport in Denver. After getting through TSA we noticed a couple whom we had met in the IVF class. They were flying home to Chicago. We invited them to have dinner with us. We shared our stories over chips, salsa, and margaritas while we waited for our flights.

Although they were younger than we were, they were experiencing secondary infertility after the birth of their son. The state of Illinois required insurance companies to pay for IVF. They were hopeful Dr. Schoolcraft would be able to help them, since other fertility clinics had not given them much hope. We exchanged addresses and became friends on Facebook.

I was so happy to get home to see Aidan. It had only been two days, but I missed him terribly. We had left him with both of his doting grand-mothers, who had come to stay at our house. I had left detailed instruc-tions about his schedule along with a daily love note counting down the days until we would be back.

Aidan loved staying with his grandmothers because he got so much attention, but also because they took him shopping. When he was obsessed with all things John Deere, they would often go to the local trac-tor supply store.

Two days after our return, Katie, my nurse at CCRM, called back to say all of my tests were normal. They felt very strongly they could help us. We were thrown a curveball two weeks later when Katie called to report that tests had identified a deficiency in Dirk's sperm.

This was an "Aha!" for me. All these years, an abnormality in Dirk's sperm may have been a contributing factor to my miscarriages and not one of the doctors had mentioned it. I couldn't believe none of the other specialists we had seen had thought to test Dirk.

Katie explained that the issue with Dirk's sperm could be rectified through genetic testing and that Dr. Schoolcraft remained confident there was a path forward for us.

"We're going to start you on the pill. Then we'll start you on a pro-tocol in December."

I didn't have any hesitation whatsoever as I wrapped up my conver-sation with Katie. I was ready to go. I was all in.

My most important role was mom and wife, but the youthful, fun-loving part of me was still there too. In just two months the next year of my life would be laid out in front of me. Months of daily fertility medi-cations, followed by a series of medical procedures at CCRM in Denver and then, if God was willing, a pregnancy.

Knowing this, I felt that a last hurrah in Vegas with Stacy was in order. It was a spontaneous decision, but Stacy was able to make it happen. Rennie was down for being Mister Mom for a long weekend.

Stacy and I both loved dancing, so after checking into our room at the Wynn, we had a nice dinner. We whooped it up at a club that played old school hip-hop and disco. The whole weekend we both felt like we were twenty-one again.

We were out every night until three in the morning, then came home and collapsed on our beds. We slept in late and had breakfast in bed. We spent one morning lounging in bed watching "This is Forty." Stacy was a few years younger than I but I had reached that milestone age about a month before our trip. Neither one of us had ever lied about age to our gynecologists the way one of the characters had in the movie. We also hadn't ever busted our husbands for "hiding out" in the bathroom with their iPads to get some alone time. Still, we couldn't stop laughing at the characters in the movie, whose lives were strangely resonant with our own.

I never would have imagined that I would start my forties on fertility drugs, but I did. Spiritually I was in the best possible place I had ever been, so I didn't have any inner turmoil about where I found myself.

It took me a week to recoup from our girls' weekend. Even though I felt young while we were there, it was clear that I wasn't twenty-one anymore. When my first shipment of medications from Dr. Schoolcraft arrived, I was so glad I had taken that weekend to have some fun. The box was enormous—the size of a large moving box. I almost passed out when I opened it and saw a packet of about a hundred syringes. "Oh my gosh," I thought as I started unloading all of the sterilized contents. It was quickly filling up our kitchen counter, where I could usually set out our Thanksgiving turkey and nine side dishes. I made up my mind right then and there that it was not good for me to see it.

Even though I had texted a picture to Dirk earlier in the day, his jaw dropped when he came home and saw our counter overflowing with medical supplies. He was brilliant at organizing and being methodical. I knew I needed him to take charge and manage the process for me.

"Honey, I need you to handle this for me."

Our growth as a couple was so evident in the moment. Dirk listened empathetically and gave me what I needed emotionally in that moment.

"I'm on it."

The very next night we began the protocol as a team. Dirk had organized all of the syringes and medications and put everything away where I wouldn't see them. I stayed in our bedroom praying while he prepped the six syringes of various hormones in the kitchen. With the cross that Pastor Linda had given me in my hands, I read Philippians 4:13 out loud: "I can do all things through Christ who strengthens me."

Once the injections were ready, I went into the kitchen. Dirk and I wrapped our arms around one another and prayed together. We asked God to help the drugs do what they needed to do without the horrible side effects I had experienced before. After praising God and thanking him, Dirk administered the various injections clockwise in my abdomen. That was for two reasons: first, to minimize bruising, and second, so that the dark purple bruises would indicate where he had given the shot last. Once he was finished, I also had pills to swallow and had four patches of estrogen to place on my arms.

This was our routine twice a day, every day, for a month. At a different point in our marriage it could have been a horribly difficult time for us. Strangely, everything we had been through as a couple had made us more connected. The work we had done in therapy had broken down walls and opened up our hearts to one another in ways that created a true partnership. Sometimes Dirk would even joke, "Whatever this is, let's keep you on it."

God's blessings were all around us. We unexpectedly found ourselves in the sweetest and most tender time of our marriage. We had prayed that the medications would bring me great joy and bring us closer together as a couple, and they had. It was nothing short of miraculous, my friends. God had listened to everything we had asked for and taken it five steps further.

CHAPTER 26

This Is Forty

From start to finish, the protocol of fertility injections and drugs lasted five and a half weeks. At the end of the fifth week, Dirk and I flew back to Denver, where I could be monitored by Dr. Schoolcraft and his medical staff at CCRM. During those last few days, I continued the injections and had daily blood work and ultrasounds to determine when I would receive the final shot that would trigger my eggs to mature to their final stage.

It was all business during the day. Then at night, Dirk and I had "couples time" together. We had nice dinners and went to the movies. Despite all of the unknowns, it was the closest we had ever been—and we were both enjoying it. My sweet friend Libbi sent me flowers with a card that read "Go, ovaries, go!" and I also received some from my sister. I felt loved and supported!

One night after dinner, my nurse Katie called as we were walking in to see *The Hunger Games*. As usual, she sounded very positive.

"Dr. Schoolcraft looked at your blood work and ultrasounds. He would like you to take the day off tomorrow and get your hCG trigger shot the day after."

It felt a little weird to get this big news right before walking into a movie theater, but I didn't worry. We had been guided here by God and had been given positive medical feedback. Still, I had a rush of adrenaline and my heart was beating fast as the lights dimmed and the movie began.

The trigger shot (also known as a STIM shot) was just enormous. It had been shipped to us in the second box of medications, and we had taken it to Denver with us. Giving me the STIM shot was a formidable task because of the unbelievable size of the syringe. CCRM required Dirk to watch a video and do a tutorial that had him practice on an orange.

Two nights later, Dirk and I were ready for our big moment. We had come such a long way from the night he gave me the very first injection. Tonight we laughed about it together. I "dropped trou" and stuck out my derriere.

I could tell Dirk was a little nervous. The pressure was on. I didn't want to see the size of the needle, but I accidentally caught a glimpse of it in the corner of my eye. I held my breath and tightened my grip on the wooden cross in my hand. Dirk cleaned off the site, pinched my skin, and counted it down. The injection was painful and stung a bit. Instead of the burning lasting three to four seconds like the others, it was somewhere between seven and ten seconds.

Dirk got it on the first try—and we were both so relieved. We hugged one another and prayed. We thanked God for all of the blessings and for the experience of bringing us closer together. We asked him to guide Dr. Schoolcraft's hands during the egg retrieval surgery.

The following morning I checked into CCRM at 7 a.m. My stomach was grumbling because I had fasted. I was a bit dismayed when Katie told me Dr. Schoolcraft would actually not be the one performing the procedure. "Well, okay," I thought as I changed into the gown. There were no guarantees about the number of eggs they would be able to harvest. I had just turned forty a few months before, so I had to accept the biological limitations imposed by my age. CCRM was a well-oiled machine, so I had to trust in their practices. Ultimately, I knew the outcome was in God's hands.

The surgery was so fast that I spent more time in the recovery room than I did in the actual surgery. Dirk's face was the first thing I saw when I opened my eyes. The anesthesia made me groggy, but I had no trouble when he told me that the surgeon had retrieved numerous viable eggs from my ovaries. I smiled as Dirk high-fived me.

"Good job, honey."

I was so proud of my little body. Despite my "ripe old age" (in the fertility world) of forty, it had gotten through the hard part and exceeded expectations.

It turned out being forty didn't feel the way I imagined it would when I was in my twenties. I was wiser and had experienced growth I never knew I was capable of.

Dirk and my sister threw me a *Real Housewives* themed fortieth birthday party. The invitation was hilarious—like a magazine ad for the show. It was such a beautiful night filled with people that I loved. Some of my bridesmaids, whom I affectionately refer to as "the girls," flew in from all over the U.S. to help me celebrate.

The girls and I have been friends for more than twenty years. We all lived together in Tulsa, and we meet up annually for a girls' trip. We're all *Real Housewives* junkies, and our time together is filled with pranks, spa time, shopping, dancing, and libations. I never laugh harder than when I am with them.

In the middle of cutting the cake, I heard a ruckus outside in the lobby. My sister said, "The girls are fighting. You better go handle it."

I walked out to find Tracey and Masha arguing. Although they are both headstrong attorneys, I had never seen them like this. Masha had her shoe in her hand, and they were practically screaming at each other.

"You have been staring me down all night! I am sick of it!"

I stood there listening for a few minutes and had to step in.

"Girls. Seriously? At my fortieth birthday party? We are together for forty-eight hours and you can't get along?"

I turned around to find a crowd gathering behind me watching the show. Tracey looked at Masha and they both started laughing.

"Gotcha!" she said.

"I mean, it's a *Real Housewives* themed party so we thought staging a fight was a must."

We all laughed and went back into the party and danced the night away.

That next month, I decided to bid on a photo package from a boudoir studio at a fundraiser. Normally, I would never entertain dressing scantily clad and posing for photos, but now that I had turned forty—I changed my mind. Thanks to all the Pilates I did, my body was in the best shape it would ever be in. Hopefully, a few months from now I would be pregnant and not have this kind of time on my hands for a while. I couldn't stop smiling as I walked into the studio. I felt very bold as I scheduled my appointment for the following week.

It was snowing on the day of the photo shoot. I didn't tell Dirk what I was doing because I was going to surprise him with a book of photographs for Valentine's Day. The photo session was so much fun. I had bought a bra and panties for one set of photos and a fur vest and a cute little gold sequined dress for the other. Mind you, I wasn't going to pose naked. Someday, Aidan would have to clean out my photo albums after I was gone. I didn't want to scar the poor kid.

I chuckled at the thought of him running across photos of his forty-year-old mother—scantily clad. I was a bit nervous but the photographer had all of the poses down. My hair and makeup were professionally done. I didn't feel awkward at all—I felt confident. One of the side effects of the hormone injections was how curvy it had made my body, so I felt really sexy.

Toward the end of the session, the snow was really coming down. Through the window I saw the beautiful flakes of snow falling from the late afternoon sky. They were so big they didn't look real. I quickly turned to the photographer.

"Can we go outside?"

It seemed a little crazy to step outside into the alleyway in the thirty-degree air wearing only a little gold sequined dress, a fur vest, and stilettos, but it was worth it. The snowflakes fell all around me. It was an unexpectedly beautiful moment.

I was so overwhelmed with emotion when I saw the photographs that I actually cried. They were absolutely stunning. I was far from perfect, but I felt the best about myself I ever had. I truly loved myself for who I was and maybe for the first time, I loved my body.

It may have taken forty years but finally, at long last, I felt like I had grown up.

CHAPTER 27

Life Suspended

Several weeks after my eggs had been retrieved, we received the happy news we'd been waiting for. The procedure had yielded a handful of healthy embryos. The next step would be to transfer the embryos back into my uterus. But first, my body would get a much needed two-month break from fertility drugs and procedures.

Coincidentally, it was Aidan's spring break and was the perfect time to get away. I found a charming little motel in Key Largo with hammocks on the beach. We spent five days there swimming and enjoying the warm sun. As I watched Aidan playing in the white sand, I was hopeful that this time next year we would have a newborn baby. Aidan was already six, and was so ready to be a big brother.

It was confusing to him that he didn't have a sibling. He didn't like being an only child and asked me all the time why he didn't have a brother or a sister. Through all of our ups and downs, we had kept everything as normal as possible for him and had never so much as alluded to my miscarriages.

Aidan also wanted to know why God wasn't answering his nightly prayers. This was a difficult question to be confronted with. I encouraged him to continue praying and told him I trusted that God would deliver. In true six-year-old fashion, Aidan responded by standing up in his bed and yelling his prayers to the ceiling to make sure God could hear him.

"GOD! CAN YOU HEAR ME? I WANT A BROTHER OR A SISTER! WHY AREN'T YOU LISTENING TO ME?"

It was so painful to watch.

Two and half weeks after our return from Florida I began the drug protocol to prep my body for the embryo transfer. One of the primary functions of the drugs was to thicken the endometrial lining of my uterus so the embryo could attach. This time around, I had hormone patches, supplements, and suppositories in addition to the daily injections. By the second week of injections, my belly was purple and brown. As he did before, Dirk would rotate the injection site in a clockwise pattern. Although I was bruised and sore, I felt great.

Dirk and I were a well-oiled machine at this point. We continued to pray together after every set of injections. We specifically prayed that God would prepare my body to receive the embryo. We would remind ourselves that God knew our heart's desires. I was so grateful that I didn't feel hormonal at all; I actually felt euphoric.

Dr. Schoolcraft needed to know how my body was reacting to the drugs, so I was monitored locally by Dr. Craig. Every week I went in for blood work to measure my hormone levels. As the date of the transfer approached, I was required to go in for several consecutive days in a row for blood work. All of my numbers were right on target. There were all indications that the lining of my uterus was thickening and was developing the characteristics it needed for the embryo to stay attached. My hormone levels were just where Katie wanted them to be. The way my body was responding to the meds was so encouraging.

It was late spring by this time—and around me there was new life. The tulips in our front yard were in full bloom. The new season had also brought with it the beautiful Oklahoma sunrises that painted the sky with the most gorgeous shades of pink, purple, and orange.

Before we knew it, it was time to fly back to CCRM for the transfer. We were up very early the morning of our flight to Denver. We had been on this long road for the better part of the year and it was finally leading up to the big moment. Along the way, we had to make the important decision of how many embryos to transfer. I was well aware that multiple embryos increased our chances of success, but my intuition told me to transfer only one embryo. This was crystal clear to me, and Dirk trusted my instincts.

Our journey also had its comedic moments, which included transporting our fertility drugs to Denver with us. In addition to our massive binder, CCRM had given us a small Styrofoam cooler to carry on board our flight. Dirk and I couldn't help but laugh at ourselves as we made our way through the TSA line with our cooler full of fertility drugs and documentation signed by Dr. Schoolcraft.

We had a full five days in Denver before the transfer. I went to CCRM daily to have blood work done and ultrasounds to measure my lining. This information would be critical to know exactly when to do the transfer. Once again, our nights consisted of going to the movies and quiet dinners.

Finally, it was the morning of the transfer. I was allowed to eat breakfast, but could not have caffeine. After Dirk gave me the last fertility injection, I sat down to drink a bottle of water so I could go into the procedure with a full bladder. Apparently the full bladder would lift my pelvis and give optimal visualization of my uterus during the procedure.

I was still chugging down the last of my water bottle when Dirk and I arrived at CCRM. We were both relatively calm, considering our agenda for the morning. Dirk, as always, had his newspaper and his cup of decaf coffee. I clenched my pocket cross in the palm of my hand. I was so thankful to be here. *This was it!*

Once we were in the sterilized room, I changed into a gown and hospital socks. Dirk was given a surgical mask and scrubs to wear during the procedure. The nurse then took us through formalities regarding ownership of the embryos. As I signed and initialed the agreements, I couldn't help thinking about how I needed to pee. She gave me a Valium—which of course was glorious.

After a few minutes, Dr. Schoolcraft marched in. Behind him was the embryologist with a rolling incubator that had a microscope, camera, and monitor attached. They were both wearing blue scrubs and surgical masks. I couldn't see the embryologist's face behind the mask, but I could see that he was young. I was so in awe of both of them. They weren't just doctors, they were scientists. I marveled that the embryologist had met our embryo before we had. They had taken my egg and fertilized it with Dirk's sperm, grown it to five days and ten cells, then froze it. It was life suspended.

I lay down on the exam table. The embryologist stepped forward and made eye contact with me.

"The thawing process went very well. Would you like to see your embryo?"

I was in disbelief as Dr. Schoolcraft turned on the monitor. There on the screen was our five-day-old baby floating in fluid. It was so miraculous—I had no words. It was such a profound moment we had to document it. We took pictures of the embryo on the screen and posed for pictures with Dr. Schoolcraft. I couldn't help myself—I cried.

Before proceeding, Dr. Schoolcraft had some serious words for us.

"Now you understand you've chosen to transfer one embryo, so you only have a forty percent chance of success."

I nodded my head as I spoke. "I understand." Dr. Schoolcraft's caution did not concern me at all. I felt in my heart that transferring just the one embryo was the right thing to do. He looked at me in acknowledgment of my decision, then continued.

"This is embryo 5AB. It is the most viable and has the greatest chance of success."

I felt the pressure on my full bladder as he used the speculum to open me up. The transfer catheter felt cold against my skin as he inserted it and injected the embryo into my uterus. I could tell that Dr. Schoolcraft had high hopes and expectations that the transfer would be a success.

"Here we go. Oh, this looks wonderful. Very good."

Even though my bladder was about to burst, I had to lie flat on the exam table for the next hour. Dirk and I said a few prayers, but in the end I needed Dirk to distract me from my urge to get up and run to the bathroom. After the sixty minutes were up, I jumped off the table, changed my clothes, and sprinted to the ladies room.

I spent the next forty-eight hours lying flat in my hotel room. We were always so busy at home that honestly it was nice being still for a change. Aidan was back at home with his two doting grandmothers, Nana and Nene.

Once I was back home, I kept looking for signs that I might be pregnant. Although the hormones I had been on the last month made me feel "elevated" in my mood, I didn't feel pregnant. But it was early. On the twelfth day, I went into the lab and took a pregnancy test. I had become friendly with the technicians who worked there. They knew what I had gone through and were so hopeful for me. A day later Katie called me. My heart raced when I saw her number pop up on my phone.

"You're pregnant!"

I squealed with delight. I called Dirk to share the news: "This is it!" We were just absolutely over the moon. We were grateful and relieved. After the added pressure of travel and expenses and yet no guarantee, it was such a great feeling. With the ICSI procedure and genetic testing, we were confident that this time would be it. Dirk told me that he loved me and gave a "Yahoo!" as we hung up.

CHAPTER 28

Foot on the Brake

Dirk and I were on cloud nine after finding out we were pregnant. As joyful as we were, this was not our first rodeo, so we didn't want to let our minds go too far. Our last six pregnancies had ended within the first trimester, so we both had some trepidation. Dr. Schoolcraft had already cautioned us that since we had done IVF, we had learned of our pregnancy weeks earlier than we normally would have. We had a strict schedule of blood work so he could monitor us very closely. None of our previous doctors or specialists had done this, so it made me feel more confident.

Since it was still so early, I felt hormonal—but not pregnant. I continued taking several hormones including shots, pills, and four estrogen patches. All things considered, I was feeling great. Still, I had my foot on the brake. I knew I needed to bring my cheerleaders along for the ride.

A small group of my best girlfriends knew we had done IVF, and they had been incredibly supportive all these months. Stacy and Melissa were on the journey with us and were my "rocks" during the entire process. Melissa, who was Catholic, always kept us in her prayers and lit candles for us at her church. Even Ben, who doesn't attend mass on a regular basis, lit a candle for us. It made us feel so loved and supported. My Sunday school friends Valerie and Melanie, who were experiencing secondary infertility, were also sending up prayers and sending positive thoughts to us. To have their support meant everything. They really "got it."

I was being monitored locally by Dr. Craig, so three days after the initial blood work I went to the lab to repeat it. Katie called later that afternoon while I was folding laundry in the bedroom. She was very happy and encouraging.

"These are really strong numbers."

The enthusiasm in her voice prompted my curiosity.

"What does that mean? Did the embryo split?"

"I'm not going to say at this point. We won't know for several weeks."

I was giddy with excitement. Thrilled and overwhelmed all at once at the thought that I might be carrying twins. I immediately called Dirk to share the good news. He was on-top-of-the-world excited.

Three days later I returned to the lab to repeat the blood work again. Like clockwork, Katie called me later that afternoon with a report. I happened to be at Dirk's office working with his assistant. Katie sounded very positive.

"We got your numbers back. They have tripled."

I kind of laughed. "Wow. So that's good?"

"Well . . . these aren't typical numbers. It's very likely that it's twins. Dr. Schoolcraft wants to keep an eye on this. We're going to check you again. If it normalizes you're okay. But if it triples again, there's a concern."

I was excited and a little scared about the possibility of twins. Once again, God had inserted humor into my life just the way he had with Aidan's platinum blond hair. Dirk had wanted to transfer two embryos, but I had been adamant about only transferring one.

I ran over to his office and found him at his desk.

"So much for transferring only one." Dirk looked up at me and I added, "They think it's twins!" A smile spread across his face. We both laughed, knowing the joke was on me. God had a different plan for us.

We knew we had to be careful about making ourselves vulnerable by sharing our news. There had already been a lot of heartbreak and we certainly didn't want to bring anyone on an emotional roller coaster again.

The last time we had included our Sunday school class in our happy news, my pregnancy turned out to be ectopic. This time around, I wasn't quite through my first trimester, but we needed prayer. We took a leap of faith and decided to tell our class the very next Sunday.

It was a beautiful late spring day and I was wearing a cute little silk dress. I obviously wasn't showing yet, so there was no way anybody would have known. When we walked into the classroom, there were already four other couples sitting in a circle. I looked around and thought, "These are the people that are supposed to hear." I settled into my seat. Dirk took the lead. He cleared his throat nervously before he spoke.

"So, Steph and I have some news. We've gone thru IVF. We started in January and just went through the embryo transfer. Steph is pregnant." The class was genuinely happy for us. There was a lot of exhaling, hugging and congratulations. At the end of the class one of the husbands prayed over the pregnancy. We all joined hands in a circle and prayed for our baby. It felt so good to include them.

Later that week I repeated my blood work. This was the test that would completely change the trajectory of my life. The lab technicians knew something was different this time around and wished me luck as I sat down.

It just so happened that when Katie called that afternoon, I was at Dirk's office again. My hands were clammy as I answered my cell phone. I could immediately tell by Katie's tone that something was wrong.

"Steph, it's Katie. Your numbers have more than tripled again."

I instantly felt sick to my stomach and my heart started pounding.

"So what does that mean?"

"We think we could be looking at a molar pregnancy."

I had no idea what that was. Katie continued.

"There is a possibility of twins or triplets but these numbers look dangerous and abnormal. Doctor Schoolcraft wants to wait and see. We won't need to repeat blood work. The next step will be an ultrasound in ten days."

I experienced a whole gamut of emotions as I hung up the phone with Katie. I felt like I had vertigo as I made my way to Dirk's office. He looked like I had kicked him in the gut when I told him the grim news. Somehow, he managed to be calming even though his eyes showed the sadness and confusion he was feeling.

"Hang tight. We don't know what's going on yet."

I had already Googled the definition of molar pregnancy and knew it was the result of the abnormal growth of tissue within the uterus. Abnormal tissue growth was of course another way of saying cancer.

I was terrified, and couldn't help but feel guilty for going public with our pregnancy. Once again, we had inadvertently dragged our families and friends on a roller coaster that was in danger of going off the tracks. I also felt guilty about the time and money we had invested in the IVF procedure, only to have this pregnancy threatened just like the others.

I was having a thousand thoughts all at once. The most important of them was that I had to have hope for these babies inside of me. We had been prayerful and had clarity up until this point, but now there were no answers. Despite this, I had to hang on to hope.

It was time to pick up Aidan from school. I had one last good cry before he climbed into the car. It was raining, but I kept my sunglasses on as I drove to my mom and dad's house. The stormy weather was a perfect match for what was going on in my heart. I could tell that my mom was surprised to see us when we walked in. She was on the couch watching one of her soaps. Aidan ran over to her and gave her a big, sweet hug. I had to be careful about what I said in front of Aidan, but I needed to tell her what was going on.

"Mom, I just got news that this does not look good."

My mom's eyes filled with tears. She extended her arms and held me. I sobbed.

"You've been through enough."

After about an hour or so the rain finally let up. Aidan of course wanted to go outside and play. I needed some fresh air, so I went outside with him. He had just lost his first tooth and was wearing his rain boots, which were decorated with monkeys. He looked adorable as he jumped around in the puddles, smiling at me with that gap between his teeth.

As I watched him splash around, I had flashbacks to each of my six pregnancies. Sitting there on the front steps of my parents' porch is when I recognized for the first time that Aidan was a genuine miracle. All this time I hadn't known any different.

"Maybe I am just supposed to count my blessings," I thought to myself. I was already blessed by being mommy to this precious little boy. "What the hell am I doing?" Each pregnancy had become more dangerous than the last, and now we were talking about the possibility of cancer. I had exhausted my mind, my body, and my spirit, and now there was a chance of leaving Aidan without a mother. A voice in my head told me if this pregnancy didn't work out, it was time to hang it up.

This was the first time I had been pregnant and had access to so much data on myself. None of the other doctors and specialists had ever monitored my blood values during the early stages of my pregnancies. When I got home that afternoon, I pulled out a file box with my medical records and compared the numbers. I found that my hCG levels were usually higher than normal in my pregnancies.

I also read through the notes written by each of the doctors. The first specialist we saw noted "mild undulation of the uterine cavity may represent postsurgical change." I wasn't exactly sure what he meant, but what he seemed to be saying was that my uterus may have been permanently damaged by the C-section I had when Aidan was born. I hadn't thought about it at the time. I had trusted Dr. Allison and never considered possible consequences of a C-section three weeks earlier than Aidan's due date. If the specialist thought this might have been an issue in my recurrent miscarriages, why hadn't he said anything to us?

Dr. Hansen was onto something as well. In his notes, he wrote that all of my pregnancies had been very early and that perhaps all of them had been ectopic. He attributed this to what he referred to as my "advanced age." I was then in my mid to late thirties and had never considered that I was "old." All these years my body had been rejecting embryos, and it seemed there were some clues in the medical notes. I had to wonder why in the hell none of the doctors had elected to share this information with us.

Even after going through all of the medical records, I was still hopeful for a miracle. Stacy and Rennie had been by our side through all of our ups and downs. When we called them to tell them my pregnancy was in jeopardy, they came right over. We all sat on the couch together and Rennie prayed over us for what seemed like thirty minutes. Although I was terrified, I also felt very much like God was by my side. I felt so blessed to have Dirk, Rennie, and Stacy holding my hand.

The next five days were complete agony. I desperately wished that I could fast-forward time to the day of the ultrasound. Walking into Sunday school that morning, I felt like I had a dark cloud over my head. Dirk and I had already agreed not to share the latest development with the class until Dr. Schoolcraft confirmed things one way or another. We decided that until then, we would just ask for continued prayer.

I did my best to put on a brave face and focus on our discussion of Paul. Twenty minutes into the class, I felt cramping.

"No."

"No f'ing way," I thought to myself.

I sat there for a minute and shifted in my seat. I was cautiously relieved when the cramping went away. But within five minutes it returned. It was the same familiar foe I had felt all those years ago in the mall when I had my first miscarriage. I tried my best not to panic, and excused myself from the class.

The carpet felt slippery under my heels as I strode across the twenty steps to the bathroom.

"Please God, please God, no. I am *begging* you." I prayed as I lifted up my dress and sat down on the toilet seat. I opened my eyes, looked down, and there it was in the water—bright red blood, tissue, blood clots, and flakes of blood circling around the inside of the bowl.

I was immediately furious at God. I could not believe that I was miscarrying—in church. It felt like a damn slap in the face. It was everything I could do to stop myself from raising my face toward the ceiling and shouting, "You guided me here! And this is how it's going to end?"

I felt no other emotion but anger. The sound of my breath amplified in my ears as I shoved toilet paper in my underwear and stormed out of the bathroom. I threw my purse on a pew outside the Sunday school classroom and yanked the door open. Everyone turned to look at me standing in the doorway. I looked at Dirk, seething.

"We need to go. I'm miscarrying."

Dirk jumped up.

"What do you mean? What is going on?" he asked.

"We have to leave!" I didn't wait to see the reactions from our friends in class.

We couldn't discuss anything on the way home because we had Aidan in the car. Instead, I slipped on my sunglasses and resigned myself to my happy mommy voice.

"What are we going to have for lunch, Mommy?

"Leftovers, sweetie."

Dirk could tell I wouldn't be able to maintain the uplifting voice, so he jumped in and chatted with Aidan on the rest of the ride home.

As soon as we got home, I marched into our bedroom and threw away the bloody toilet paper that I had used to line my underwear. I purposefully pulled out the "granny panties" I had bought all those years ago when I had my first miscarriage and put on a sanitary pad. I stood in the bathroom at the sink, feeling numb as I rinsed out my underwear.

I had already put in a call to the weekend nurse at CCRM and was anxiously waiting for a call back. Dirk decided to take Aidan out to the farm, so I was alone. The house was deathly quiet. I was trying to process everything that was happening. I had miscarried before, but this time it was different. It was more painful, and I could actually feel my body passing large blood clots. To make matters worse, I had horrific guilt about all the money we had poured into this pregnancy.

With every minute that passed I felt rage building inside me. I felt completely betrayed by God. How could this have happened on His watch? I grew so livid that I screamed and threw something against the bedroom wall. The ringing of my phone reeled me back in. It was Pastor Linda. I had texted her on the way home from church.

Linda was truly shocked. It felt comforting to know that if she was upset, it was okay for me to be upset with God. She prayed over the phone.

"We do not understand why this is happening. We are heartbroken. Please help Stephanie and hold her in the palm of your hand, Lord. She needs to know that you are here. Let her feel Your presence."

Finally, the weekend nurse at CCRM called me back. I briefed her on everything that was happening. She was very calm.

"You can do one of two things. We can do a blood draw or we can set up a D&C."

As she spoke, I couldn't help thinking about all of these months of medications, injections, blood work, and time spent away from Aidan.

Now I had to confront this pregnancy ending like all of the others. I didn't want any more surgeries and it wasn't worth it to me to be put under yet again. I had done it both ways and in either case, it was a long, heart-breaking good-bye. And as graphic as it sounds, no matter what choice I made, I would still bleed.

CHAPTER 29

Trial by Fire

For days afterward, I was in grief mode. I was struggling to reconcile my faith and my feelings of being mad at God. I felt so let down by Him! He had guided me, put me on a path to the highest mountain peak, and then let me tumble down. My eyes filled with tears as I yelled at the ceiling.

"You guided me here! *Why?*"

I wanted so desperately to know why. Why had He let this happen to me?

I was also in quite a bit of physical pain. I was still bleeding and cramping—literally losing my pregnancy bit by bit. I was so exhausted mentally that once I got Aidan off to his summer day camp, all I wanted to do was sleep, cry, and watch mindless television on Bravo.

My devotional that morning was on Peter 1:7. "These trials will show that your faith is genuine. It is being tested as fire tests and purifies gold." I knew this was true. I didn't believe God was abandoning me. But I was still mad at Him.

I was confused and uncertain as to why God wasn't delivering my prayers. But, I knew He was going to work on my behalf. I felt forgotten, but I also knew in my heart that I had to trust in His perfect timing. While we all wait for our prayers, it can be hard to see God. And it certainly was in this moment.

Sweet Pastor Linda was right there with me. She called to check on me and I told her exactly how I was feeling. She listened thoughtfully as the words spilled out of my mouth, then gave me her perspective.

"You may never understand. And Stephanie, it's okay to be mad at God. So take the time you need and when you are ready, ask Him for some peace while you wait on Him."

When I finally came out of the darkness, I was glad I had taken her advice and let myself be incensed for a few days. By the end of the third day, I was ready to get outside for some fresh air. Even though I hadn't washed my hair in a couple of days, I asked Dirk to take me for a ride in his convertible. The Cutlass was from the year he was born and was one of his prized possessions. He had looked long and hard to find it.

We took it for countless long cruises on date nights and even drove it in the town Christmas parade with Aidan a few times. I had so many special memories in that car that I knew it was the perfect way to breathe some life back into my spirit.

It was only a fifteen-minute cruise down the highway, but the wind in my hair and fresh air felt so good. I looked over at my sweet hubby. It was so good to see him smiling and to have him at my side. This was definitely the worst moment of our infertility journey, but this time we struggled *together* to process what had happened, and our crisis had brought us even closer. I was so thankful that it wasn't doing the opposite.

Still, I knew it wasn't over. I knew that God wouldn't lead us down this path and abandon us. We just weren't sure what our next steps would be. Stacy had come right over when I miscarried and sat on my bed with me. She told me once again that the offer she had made to carry my baby still stood. I was so touched, but I was so emotional that I couldn't even process her words. I thanked her and told her we were so appreciative of the offer. I was in shock that she brought it up again—and couldn't believe I had a friend who would actually do that for me.

That Friday afternoon, Dirk and I were in our bedroom. I was scrolling through Facebook and Dirk was going through some mail when he got a call on his cell. I had no idea who he was talking to, but the conversation went downhill quickly.

"Why was the garage door open? Did you call the police?"

I knew then he was talking to my parents. We kept the Cutlass in their extra garage and it sounded like something bad had happened. Dirk was ready to jerk someone bald when he hung up the phone.

"Your parents were in the backyard cleaning out the hot tub and they forgot to close the garage door. My convertible is gone."

I felt so sad for Dirk, and even worse because my parents were to blame. We immediately headed over to their house. My mom was very apologetic when we arrived. I couldn't believe she hadn't called the police yet. I had a friend who was a cop, so I immediately called him. He was ready to help and wasted no time getting details.

"What color is it?

"Red."

The car was so unique that I knew it wouldn't be hard to track it down, along with the perpetrators. Dirk came back outside and overheard the last part of my conversation.

"Who are you on the phone with?"

"The police."

"Here, I will talk to them."

He took my phone. I was even more confused now.

I sat on the same porch step where I had watched Aidan jump in the rain puddles. I put my face in my hands and cried. I couldn't take more loss at this moment.

All of a sudden, I heard a horn start honking in the distance. The sound grew closer and closer. I looked up just as the rumble of the engine reached my ears and saw our Cutlass suddenly appearing at the corner of the cul-de-sac. I couldn't tell who was driving, but the hooligans were wearing sunglasses, towels, and bandanas on their heads. What in the hell?

As they approached, I saw that it was my dad behind the wheel—but I couldn't tell who the other three people were. The car pulled up into the driveway, stopped, and they took off their disguises. It was "the girls!" My sister Melanie, Tracey, Masha, and Linda all piled out of the car and ran over to give me a hug. They were all laughing. I couldn't believe they were all here. I fell to my knees and sobbed.

"We got you!" Tracey said.

I was so confused and relieved that Dirk's car wasn't stolen. And of course, I was so happy to see my best girls.

"What are you doing here?"

The girls just laughed and gave me the biggest hugs. I couldn't believe they had pulled off this elaborate prank. They had never seen me in the midst of my miscarriages. Tracey lived in Atlanta, Masha lived in Pittsburgh, and Linda and Melanie lived in Dallas. Melanie had organized the entire thing except for the prank. It had Tracey's fingerprints all over it.

I ugly-cried for a good five minutes. They had demanding jobs and I knew how difficult it was for them to get away, especially on a moment's notice. I was so touched that they had dropped everything to come see me. And I realized that I really needed them at that exact moment.

We went inside and popped open a bottle of champs. I couldn't stop smiling at them. I felt so blessed. I had been in such a severe depression; it felt so good to smile.

"Let's go sing karaoke. I'll do my best 'Baby Got Back,'" my sister said.

"I already have my song picked out!" Tracey said.

I looked like a hot mess. The thought of going to a karaoke bar in my state, even if it was a hole in the wall, was unimaginable. I negotiated a few minutes to clean myself up. I had been having such a terrible time making the shift out of the grief; these girls were the shot in the arm I needed.

CHAPTER 30

Purgatory

The Monday morning after the girls left, I reentered reality with a drive to the lab for blood work. This was my third trip to the lab since my miscarriage to have my hormone levels checked. My hCG level needed to level out to zero for my pregnancy to be officially over and for my body to be considered "normal" again. I was looking forward to feeling like my usual self again, but for now I was weepy.

This miscarriage was different from the others. This time around I was mourning not just the loss of my baby, but also the dream of ever having another pregnancy. I was having so many feelings, and I had just as many questions. Why was my body rejecting my babies? How did my undiagnosed condition continue to elude even the most advanced tests? I also could not stop thinking about my sister Melanie. We shared the same DNA and yet she hadn't experienced any of the pregnancy issues that I had. I was so thankful for her health. But I was mystified as to how my body kept failing. How was this possible?

Dr. Schoolcraft was one of the top fertility doctors in the world and not even he had answers to these questions. He had called me the day after my miscarriage and was surprisingly empathetic and comforting. He also made it very clear that my best chance for having more children was through a gestational carrier. I could hear the surprise in his voice when I told him my best friend had offered to be my carrier.

A week later when Stacy stopped by, I still wasn't ready to explore the idea. Stacy was like a sister to me, even though we were opposites. She was very analytical, logical, and not nearly as emotional as I tended to be. She was also very decisive and known for being a solution finder at work and on the various volunteer committees we had been on together.

Tonight, she was wearing her heart on her sleeve and was very focused on solving my problem. Her eyes teared up as she reiterated her offer to carry a baby for me.

"We're best friends. We're neighbors. Let me do this for you."

I knew that God had laid this on her heart after her baby shower when she was just weeks away from giving birth to Evie. All these years later, she was still all in. I was touched beyond belief that she was offering to make such a huge sacrifice for me. I didn't have the words to express to her what this meant. Still, I was grieving and not in a place to make any decisions. I also had other serious concerns.

"I'm so worried about risking our friendship and worried about putting your health at risk." I could see that Stacy, as she always did, completely understood how I was feeling.

"Well, whenever you're ready the offer stands."

Just as we had on the car ride home from the baby shower, we cried and hugged.

I needed closure before I could move forward. Based on the results of my second round of blood work, that wasn't coming any time soon. Typically, the pregnancy hormone levels should have leveled out within a couple of weeks, but mine were still really high. I would have to repeat my blood work every other week until my pregnancy hormones dropped to zero. I felt like I was stuck in purgatory.

Dirk and I had some weighty decisions to make, but for now everything remained status quo. We had plenty of other things to focus on. Less than a year before, the Cotton Family Tsunami had moved into our neighborhood. Gigi had never been the same after her stroke and needed specialized care. We had placed her in our nursing home, where we could keep a close eye on her. She went to Heaven right after my nephew Tripp was born. My parents were still in good health, but we were aware that as they aged they would need more support from us. They had been two hours away and now, as Dirk liked to say, they were just "a two-minute phone call away."

I was also the chair of a gala fundraiser for the Chamber of Commerce at the end of the month. The committee was filled with super fun and ambitious women. Working with them was always a blast, and planning the fundraiser with them was a welcome distraction.

After two months, my pregnancy hormones were finally close enough to zero that I was released from Dr. Schoolcraft's care. We knew then that it was time for us to make some decisions. We still had frozen embryos and Stacy was willing to be our carrier. Even though the math seemed simple, we did not take the decision lightly. We spent about a week being prayerful before deciding together that if there was anyone we would want to carry our baby, it was Stacy. We were also very close with Rennie, so there was no doubt in our minds that this was our path forward.

Instead of just calling them or walking right next door to their house, we set up a couples' dinner at our favorite steakhouse, so that we could discuss taking this huge step together. I had a few butterflies in my stomach as we drove along the highway. As excited as I was to share our decision with them, I was also relieved that we were all just making small talk in the car.

Dirk and I had already agreed that we wanted to enjoy our night out with our friends. We usually had some cocktails before we ordered. We wanted things to be as normal as possible and would wait for the right moment to arise. Then we would segue into a more serious conversation about the delicate topic of surrogacy.

As we sat down at our table, the hostess handed us our menus. Rennie opened his menu wide, then looked up at me and Dirk.

"Are we having a baby, or what?"

CHAPTER 31

The Pact

Almost a year to the day from my first appointment at CCRM, I found myself sitting there in the waiting area with Stacy. It was so hard for me not to weep every time I looked at her. I still couldn't believe she was giving me and Dirk this opportunity to have another child. It was a chance we wouldn't otherwise have.

Dirk and I were amazed as I watched her waiting for her full eight hours of testing and counseling to begin. She didn't have "white coat syndrome" like I was. She was confident and knew she was supposed to do this.

I had been so worried that her acting as our gestational carrier would somehow compromise our friendship. Instead, as we made the decision and formed our pact, it did the opposite. It deepened our friendship in unimaginable ways. In the three weeks between making the decision and flying out to Denver for her one-day workup, I had taken Stacy to Vegas for her "last hurrah." I figured it was the least I could do since she would spend the next few months taking fertility drugs and shots, having procedures, and then carrying our baby for nine months.

Our weekend in Vegas was a blast. We had so much fun! We danced our hearts out, listened to live music, drank fancy cocktails, had spa time, and ate some amazing food. When people would ask us, "What brings you here?" we just giggled.

Two weeks later, Stacy passed all of her tests with flying colors and got the green light from Dr. Schoolcraft to begin her fertility protocol. I ordered her meds from a pharmacy on the East Coast, and they arrived in a large refrigerated box. She had no problem giving the injections to herself.

She held my hand through all of my fertility treatments, and now I was happy to do the same for her. We were super excited and giddy as we drove out to her OB-GYN's office for her first monitoring appointment. Coincidentally, her doctor's office was located out by the steakhouse where we had dinner and made the decision to have her carry our baby.

"So, we're not a couple," I volunteered half-jokingly to the ultrasound tech. "We're best friends."

The tech smiled and became quiet as she studied the image of Stacy's uterus on the screen. I had a bad history with silence during ultrasounds, so this made me really nervous. I could tell the tech was being cautious when she finally spoke.

"It looks like there is no progression in your lining, but we need to wait for your doctor to read it."

Stacy was puzzled. She had followed the medical protocol prescribed by Dr. Schoolcraft, so the no-yield results didn't make sense to her.

"Don't worry," I offered to her. "This is our first appointment."

True to her nature, Stacy went home and studied all of the data in the two-inch-thick binder CCRM had given her. Her next appointment was on a rainy morning typical of the fall. We shared an umbrella as we sprinted from the car to the building. I couldn't resist kidding with her in the elevator.

"Should we hold hands? I could call you 'honey.'"

"Um, no."

A few minutes later, the same tech we'd had at the last appointment started the ultrasound again. Once again, the tech spoke cautiously.

"So, I am not seeing any progression today."

"What are you measuring?" Stacy asked.

"The drugs you are on should be thickening your endometrium for the embryo transfer, but unfortunately I don't see a change in your lining yet." I could see Stacy running the calculation in her head. After four years of being on a roller coaster I had grown accustomed to doctors not having answers. The tech said they would send the ultrasound to Dr. Schoolcraft and he would advise of next steps. Stacy looked a bit defeated as she slid off the exam table, buttoned her blouse, and pulled up her pants.

As soon as the elevator doors closed, she shook her head.

"I just don't understand. I just don't understand."

Tears welled up in her eyes. My heart broke for my best friend. I had never seen her like this. She had always been in control, but today she felt like she was failing.

"I'm so sorry," she said to me.

"Don't apologize to me. You are giving us a bonus round that we never would have had. I'm so sorry that you're so sad and frustrated."

Outside it was as if a monsoon had hit. The cold wind coming off the lake made the rain blow sideways. Our umbrella offered little protection. By the time we made it to the car, we were completely soaked.

Stacy looked like she had been knocked down. Suddenly I understood how Dirk must have felt watching me all of these years. I didn't think she was failing *at all*. I wasn't thinking about myself or the baby I might not get. I felt terrible for *her*. I wanted to comfort her, but nothing I said or did seemed to help.

Later that day, a nurse from CCRM called to confirm that Stacy had not progressed. I patched Stacy through on three-way so we could take the call together. The nurse was very cheery and tried to be encouraging. She outlined a plan to change Stacy's medical protocol.

"We're going to change the meds. We will do this for three days. If your lining thickens, you'll come out here for the transfer. If you don't progress, we will try again the next month."

Stacy's emergency supply of meds arrived a few days later.

We hadn't discussed how many months she was willing to try, so I let her know that she didn't have to go through this again.

"No. I want to try again."

Not long after, I could see she didn't feel great. It was hard to watch, especially since it was Christmas time.

Except for the day Aidan was born and Dirk's wedding proposal, this was the most profound gift anyone had ever given me. I thought back to the day I had given Stacy the MAC lip gloss for her birthday at our Junior League meeting. I still laughed when I recalled the look on her face—like I was a complete moron. I knew there was no way I could ever repay her, but I wanted to give her something special for Christmas.

I wasn't exactly sure what to get, but I knew it when I saw it in the case at the jewelry store: a stunning pair of red earrings. They were so beautiful and unique. Stacy cried when she opened the box. She was so emotional, which was very uncharacteristic for her.

Stacy's next appointment was in the New Year. The mood was no longer light on our drives to see her doctor. Stacy was worried and cautious. She knew the target number her endometrial lining needed to reach, and it weighed heavily on her mind.

We had a new ultrasound technician that day. I tried in vain to bring some levity into the room.

"We're not lovers. We're best friends."

My humor was completely lost on Stacy, who only had one thing on her mind.

"What are my measurements?"

Stacy's numbers were the same as they had been two months before, when we had started. There was no change. I could see the pain on her face. She simply could not wrap her head around it.

Back in the car, Stacy was beside herself.

"I just don't get it," she sobbed. "I've been pregnant twice before without any issues. This doesn't make sense."

There were no answers, and I knew from having walked in her shoes the confusion and torment she was feeling. I would have done anything to ease her pain, but she was inconsolable, just as I had been. We both sat in the car and cried until we couldn't cry any more.

CHAPTER 32

State of Allowing

In the days following the end of Stacy's fertility treatment, I realized our journey with her was a reminder of trusting God's perfect timing. Our hearts broke for Stacy, but Dirk and I were so grateful for her selfless act. We still had a couple of embryos left, so we didn't feel it was time to give up. We had this peace and trusted that it was just not meant to be right now. Somewhere down the road there would be another opportunity— on God's time.

I couldn't believe Easter was just around the corner. I had RSVP'd to a spring luncheon sponsored by the Chamber of Commerce for women in business. As much as I welcomed a chance to see my girlfriends, I was less enthusiastic about the event itself. It seemed destined to be what I jokingly referred to as just another "rubber chicken affair." Regardless, I pulled myself together. I felt better after I put on a bit of makeup and slipped into a cute little dress. I stepped into my heels, which had collected dust, and was off.

The speaker that afternoon was a lady by the name of Jacqueline. She was a business and life coach who had been one of the lead spokespeople for Tony Robbins's organization. Despite her impressive résumé it was still hard for me to settle down, even once she had taken the podium. I was being a little naughty and kept quietly chatting with my girlfriends from the Chamber board, who were seated at the table with me.

It didn't take long for me to realize Jacqueline wasn't your average motivational speaker. She had this megawatt smile, and her ideas were about energy and emitting a high vibration. Truth be told, there was a time when I might have thought her platform was a bit weird, but today I was captivated and hung on her every word.

As I sat there listening to Jacqueline's thoughts on self-worth, we locked eyes for a moment. I knew in my gut she was another angel sent to me by God. For the last few months I had been looking for a shot in the arm to help me move forward, and here she was.

After her speech, I purposefully was the last one to have my book signed by her. I could feel the energy radiating from her as I handed her my book.

"Hi! Would you please sign my book?"

She smiled, nodded, and asked for my name.

"Do you ever do private coaching?" I asked.

"Yes, I do. What line of business are you in?"

"Oh, well . . . it's actually not for my business. It's to help me have a baby." I almost whispered.

Jacqueline looked me in the eyes and smiled. "I can do that."

I knew it probably sounded a little crazy to ask a business coach to help me have a baby, but I needed guidance. I was tired of regurgitating the past in therapy. I found Jacqueline's ideas refreshing, and her message about empowerment really resonated with me.

In my first session with her she asked me to give myself a nickname. Without hesitation, I chose "Angel Wings." I thought of all of the women that God had sent to me: Pastor Linda, Stacy, Barbara, Melissa, Val, Mel, my family, the "girls," Dr. Craig, Giuliana, and now Jacqueline.

I felt like I was eating her words by the spoonful. She had a multi-layered approach that focused on my perspective in the present time.

"What are you saying with your vibration, Angel Wings?"

I hadn't ever even heard of that term. I honestly didn't know what to say.

"Uh, my vibration? What do you mean?"

Jacqueline explained that my vibration was composed of my thoughts and feelings. They were the message I emitted to the universe about what I wanted. I immediately had a mental picture of the emotional pit I had been in.

"I've been so sad and angry."

"Is this a match to your future baby?"

Her question really hit home. I suddenly realized what a hot mess I had been. It was no wonder nothing was happening for me.

"No, I'm not a match to my baby."

"You've got to reach for higher-feeling thoughts."

Jacqueline was like my own private cheerleader. By the end of our session, I felt like she had introduced me to a whole new world and way of thinking. I could see I had a lot of work to do, but I was game.

Having consistent, mindful attention to my thoughts and feelings was easier said than done. I couldn't just flip a switch. It took a lot of courage, practice, and discipline not to go down the road of negativity. It didn't take me long to see that I didn't naturally reach for feelings that felt good. For as long as I could remember, I had always gone to worst-case scenario. This way, I always told myself, I was prepared for it. I realized that I had felt that all I was worth were those negative thoughts.

I had never thought about myself as the architect of my life or my feelings as a *choice*. I didn't realize that the universe was bringing me more of what I was choosing to focus my attention on—which was loss and negativity. Jacqueline helped me see that since I was in control of my thoughts, I should choose positive ones. Instead of envisioning the worst-case scenario for myself, I should reach for thoughts that put me at ease and in what she called a state of allowing.

After about a month of practicing being mindful, I felt like I was getting the hang of it. I could actually feel an elevation in my perspective and

I felt more worthy and deserving. As I gave loving energy to positive things instead of amplifying problems, blessings naturally flowed into my life.

My sessions with Jacqueline were always enlightening and profound. This week's conversation was no exception. She asked me an important question.

"Up until now, everything in your life has unfolded the way it was supposed to. Knowing this, what do you want, Angel Wings?"

I didn't hesitate in responding. "I want another baby."

I knew Jacqueline couldn't guarantee me a baby, just as I was acutely aware that I couldn't get pregnant again. Despite this, I knew it was time to move forward. I had taken care of my soul and replenished my heart and I felt in alignment. For the first time in my life, I felt worthy, trusting of the unknown, and capable of being the woman God had intended me to be.

I couldn't help but laugh when I sat down at my computer to Google surrogacy agencies. There were pages and pages of agencies all over the country. I clicked through to the sites and checked out ratings and reviews. I almost couldn't believe the words coming out of my mouth as I left a voicemail for one of the agencies. In fact, I laughed when I got off the phone. Dirk and I had discussed using a gestational carrier, but we had concerns about having a complete stranger carry our baby.

It was April Fool's Day when I finally told Dirk what I had been up to. I already had at least twenty profiles of possible carriers. He raised his big, thick, black eyebrows and cocked his head to the side. He opened his blue eyes as wide as they would go, then paused before he spoke.

"Can we talk about this?"

"I know it's crazy . . . "

I wasn't expecting an immediate decision from him. I knew my husband was thoughtful and prayerful. He liked to do his due diligence.

I felt like I had watched the pieces of a puzzle assemble themselves in the rearview mirror of my car. We had the wisdom of our past medical experiences, exposure to surrogacy through Stacy and of course, our frozen embryos. Dirk was definitely in the passenger seat on this ride. He was all buckled up but not ready to start the car. My hand was firmly gripping the keys in the ignition. I was ready.

CHAPTER 33

Dating Online

Dirk and I had been together for over a decade and had met the "old fashioned" way, if you will. Finding a suitable match online was a trend we had both missed out on—until now, that is. Once we had made the decision to hire a gestational carrier, we were inundated with applications. One agency sent them individually and another sent them in groups of four at a time.

I printed them all out so I could look through them thoughtfully. Ever judicious, Dirk cautioned me to consider the agency as much as the applicant. It was uncharted territory for both of us, and we didn't want to feel pressured.

We weren't just looking for someone to carry our baby. It was so much more to us. We weren't even "looking" per se. Dirk and I were surrendering, obeying, and trusting in the direction in which we were being guided.

In the first twenty-four hours, I honestly felt like I had signed up on Tinder and was dating online. Every night I would log on to a password-encrypted site to review the profiles. They contained personal photographs and personal and private information about the applicants, including their education, health history, sex life, religion, body mass index, pregnancies, diet, and lifestyle. We in turn were required to disclose our finances, any criminal background, history of substance abuse, or any record with Child Protective Services.

I had printed out all of the applications along with their photographs so I could look them over carefully. One applicant had miscarried, so she was an immediate "no." Another applicant had vaginal herpes. Despite her seeming very sweet, I politely declined her. Another lived with a smoker. Who, I wondered, would consider her? Well, the joke was clearly on me, because all three of these women had been chosen as carriers before.

Before we started the process, I hadn't realized the places my mind would have to go as we proceeded. I wasn't bothered at all by being vetted by the agencies, but some of the questions of a more intimate nature made me laugh. I actually felt my face flush when I read over one of the questions on the online form asking how I would feel about my carrier having sex with her partner while carrying my child.

I knew people had their needs, but the thought of my baby "witnessing" that event on a regular basis was more than my imagination could handle. It also brought up a whole host of other questions regarding not just the health of our gestational carrier but the health of her sexual partner. Fortunately, Dr. Schoolcraft had strict requirements pertaining to sexual activity, so the answer to these questions fell largely in his court. His standards were strict all around. He required a low body mass index, and the candidate had to be in excellent health.

We also had our own criteria that we wanted the gestational carrier to meet. It was very important for us that she be healthy—both emotionally and physically. She needed to have prior experience as a surrogate. We wanted her to live within three hours of us so we could go to all of the doctor appointments with her. It was also crucial for us to find someone who was a Christian. Since we knew our contract with our gestational carrier would also be a contract with her whole family, it was critical for us that we find someone with healthy relationships.

I knew she would feel like a sister or a close friend on paper. I knew these were a lot of boxes to check, but I had faith and was not at all worried about finding someone.

About a week into the process, a profile came through that made me look twice. Her name was Tiffany and she lived in Dallas (where my sister lived). She had advanced degrees, was in good health, and had her own family. I couldn't believe my eyes as I read on and saw that not only had she been a surrogate before—she worked at a church and was a pastor's wife.

Tiffany's beautiful smile jumped off the page. I knew she was the one. I was so excited that I couldn't help reading through her profile several times and praying over it.

I showed Dirk the profile when he got home from work that day. I left the stack of applications on his dresser with hers on top. He looked through them as he was undoing his tie and taking off his shoes.

"Yep. She's the one."

A week later the surrogacy agency set up a conference call with Tiffany and her husband. We settled into our bed and put Dirk's cell phone on speaker. We kept Tiffany's profile right in front of us along with a list of questions we wanted to ask her. Dirk and I had already discussed our agenda for the phone call. We felt it was important for us to take a backseat on the call, so we could hear from them.

I was so excited to hear her voice on the phone. She had a bouncy, confident voice. Her Great Lakes accent was tinged with a bit of a Texas drawl. As soon as I heard her speak, I had an immediate connection with her. She was positive and loving, yet measured in a way that reminded me of Stacy.

There were so many parallels in our respective lives. Like me, Tiffany prayed about everything and had been guided by God. She and her husband, Brian, had been married for many years, and I could tell they were a very loving couple. Dirk immediately smiled when he heard that Brian had been raised on a farm, as he had.

What resonated most for us was that Tiffany was not doing this for the money. Acting as a gestational carrier was a ministry for her. She mentioned that she loved being pregnant and that her first surrogacy was twins. The biggest bonus was that Tiffany's entire church would be praying for her and our baby.

At the end of the forty-five-minute phone call we agreed to meet for lunch in Dallas. The timing could not have been more perfect, since my whole family was already planning to be in Dallas for the birth of my nephew; my sister was pregnant with another boy. Of all days, Melanie was being induced on Cinco de Mayo and had invited me to be in the room for the birth. The plan was to head over to the hospital right after meeting with Tiffany and Brian.

The morning of our drive to Dallas was absolutely crazy. I felt like I was having an out-of-body experience as I packed us up for the long car ride and overnight trip. I was trying to keep myself grounded for the meeting with Tiffany and in the right mental state for my sister's labor and delivery.

Aidan was riding with my parents in the Cotton Family Tsunami caravan. Their plan was to go straight to the hospital. As I pulled together Aidan's clothes, DVDs, colors, and treats, I had to laugh and wonder if the Tsunami would make it to Dallas in time for the birth of my nephew.

We were thrilled that we had found Tiffany, but it was still shocking that we were at this point. Dirk and I were trying not to get ahead of ourselves. I had spent the week being prayerful about her passing the necessary tests at CCRM, and about my not having feelings of jealousy. We were in a bonus round, and I was so grateful. I wanted to make sure God protected this experience with Tiffany.

Three hours later we arrived at the cute little Mexican restaurant Tiffany had suggested for lunch. The restaurant was busy and festive as the diners celebrated the holiday. Tiffany and Brian were waiting for us at the table. They smiled, got up, and we hugged briefly. She was absolutely darling. The real litmus test was that she was someone I would be friends with even if she weren't going to be carrying my baby.

The first thing she did was ask to hear our story. As we talked about our infertility journey, a few tears ran down her cheek. Once we finished, I felt that she was connected with us and wanted to help. I could tell by Dirk's facial expression that he felt the same way I did. There was no question for either one of us. Tiffany was our angel.

CHAPTER 34

Shaking the Trees

Surrogacy was still a relatively new concept, so we were on a big learning curve. Even though Tiffany had sent her medical records to Dr. School-craft as quickly as she could, for weeks the only thing we heard from CCRM were crickets. In the meantime, Dirk and I were busy checking off items on our "to do" list to keep things moving forward.

As part of our agreement, we were obligated to provide Tiffany with life and health insurance, as well as an attorney. We also needed to determine what procedures would be covered by her health care provider, and at what percentage.

Finding an attorney familiar with surrogacy licensed to practice in our state was easier said than done. Googling "surrogacy lawyer" produced few results. After meeting with one very negative "naysayer" (who made me want to jump out of my seat during the consultation and strangle her), I knew we'd have to do more research to find one whose judgment we could trust. We needed someone who would fight for us.

After finding one through a referral, we then spent the next six weeks finalizing a thirty-three-page legal agreement with Tiffany. I may not have been carrying my own child, but I learned quickly that there was a great deal of effort involved in retaining someone to do it for you.

Drafting the agreement was a rigid process in which we confronted some very heavy decisions. One minute I was taking off my toe socks at the end of Pilates class and the next minute I was reading a serious email from Dirk to our attorney about the language pertaining to the medical power of attorney.

I knew the shit was "gettin' real" when I saw the clauses regarding organ loss and actions we would be obligated to take in the event Tiffany had to go on life support. It was agonizing to think about those possibilities. At that point, I handed it all over to Dirk.

"I just can't. I need for you to handle the contract. You're the lawyer, and you are good at this sort of thing."

Dirk asked me why, and I told him that it was too much for me. I couldn't let my mind go to those places. He shook his head.

"Okay, I understand. I'm on it."

It was a very protected group who were in on our secret. We had been through so much, and we didn't want to bring anyone along on another roller coaster ride. We also wanted to protect Aidan, who had no idea about what we were up to. I cringed at the thought of running into someone at the grocery store or baseball practice who might offer congratulations in front of our unsuspecting son. With this in mind, we made a decision to only share our news with Stacy and Rennie, Melissa and Ben, and of course, our families.

My father-in-law didn't bat an eyelash when we shared our plan with him. He was a cattle rancher, so he was no stranger to reproductive engineering. In fact, he had several frozen embryos in a tank in his barn. He was a man of few words, but he did manage to get out a signature O'Hara "Woooo-hoooo!"

My mother-in-law's relief was palpable. She agreed this was the best possible route for us to take. Her big blue eyes lit up behind her glasses. She nodded her head and smiled at us as she exhaled.

I was very touched by my mother's response. Like my mother-in-law, she was visibly relieved when I told her about Tiffany. I thought it was very sweet that she wanted to get to know Tiffany. It occurred to me that it might be nice to have my mom come with us to one of the ultrasounds.

My father, of course, had his usual over-the-top reaction.

"*Damn!* How much does that cost?"

I wasn't offended by the question. I knew that once we went public with our covert operation, this would be a question on everybody's minds. The truth was, we *were* making a financial sacrifice.

We were responsible for everything from Tiffany's maternity clothes to every last unforeseen medical cost. It was a huge gamble with no guarantees, but Dirk and I didn't want to ever have any regrets. We still had frozen embryos, so we took our chances and rolled the dice.

Almost every day I had to take a deep breath and remind myself to take it all one step at a time. It had been over two months now and we hadn't heard a word from CCRM about Tiffany. I knew I needed to be patient and allow for God's perfect timing, but I also knew that God didn't want me to be passive.

After doing a little bit of detective work and shaking the trees at CCRM, I finally got Tiffany approved for a one-day workup in early October. The nurse we had been working with was on maternity leave, and her replacement was not familiar with the surrogacy side of things.

Tiffany was approved by Dr. Schoolcraft and received her schedule of meds, but because of Dr. Schoolcraft's schedule she would not be able to start treatment until December. Normally at that time of year I was looking forward to Christmas. This year I had something even more spectacular to look forward to!

Even though we were months out, CCRM was all systems go and had already scheduled lining checks and the transfer in January. Of all days, one of the lining checks was on Aidan's seventh birthday. All these years, he had been praying for a brother or a sister. After my last miscarriage his prayers had grown more ambitious, and every night he asked for a brother *and* a sister. It was gut wrenching to listen to him, but I never tried to correct him.

"Oh my *Lord*," I thought to myself as I looked up at the ceiling. "We've gone from 'or' to 'and.' I hope you can deliver big-time."

CHAPTER 35

God's Best

The farther along we got into the process, the more there was to it. We knew we didn't want to do this again. Dirk and I had been considering transferring both of our embryos for quite a while now. The fact that Tiffany had successfully carried twins was a big plus for us, and pushed us in that direction. Dr. Schoolcraft was also a proponent of transferring both embryos, since twins offered the possibility of a higher success rate.

Tiffany started the fertility drugs right around the time that I was finishing up with our Christmas decorations. I exhaled on New Year's Day when she called after her first lining check with a positive report. Dirk and I had a lot of history, so our excitement was contained. But it was different this time. There were positive affirmations all around us, which we hadn't had before. On Aidan's birthday, Tiffany went in for her second lining check and the results were favorable. As I hung up the phone with Tiffany and CCRM, I thought to myself, "This is *really* happening!"

By this point Dirk and I were well versed in our prayers. We prayed together numerous times throughout the day—and praised God and thanked him for Tiffany. We asked for favor and for a hedge of protection for Tiffany, Dr. Schoolcraft, and our embryos.

I knew that if it wasn't meant to be, adoption was the next step for us. Until then, I prayed over the powerful promise made in Psalm 113:9. "Praise the Lord! He settles the barren woman in her home as the happy mother of children."

A week later, we met Tiffany and Brian at the airport in Denver and made the drive out to Lone Tree, where CCRM was. The embryo transfer was scheduled for the very next morning, and we couldn't have been more thrilled to have the experience a second time. We were excited to meet the embryologist, see our embryos on the microscope projector, and most important, pray over our future children.

Even though the procedure was scheduled for nine-thirty in the morning, we were all required to check in before seven. Tiffany was very calm as we sat in the waiting area listening to the now familiar sounds of the waterfall. Our nurse, whom we had seen the day before when we had all come in together, stepped out from between the electronic surgical doors and called Tiffany back. The nurse knew Tiffany was our carrier and was aware that all four of us would be present for the transfer. Having been through it myself, I knew Tiffany would need a few minutes to change into her hospital gown, and I imagined she probably wanted some personal time with Brian. I smiled at the nurse to get her attention.

"We're not coming just yet. We'll wait for now."

The nurse nodded at me before disappearing behind the surgical doors with Tiffany and Brian in tow. As always, Dirk sipped his cup of decaf while reading his newspaper. After several minutes, I expected to see our nurse again, but the surgical doors didn't budge. I wondered what the delay in coming to get us could be. I was done with my coffee and ready to get in there. I knew the exam rooms were right inside the door, so it was just a matter of getting someone's attention, but with the doors sealed shut, I knew I would just have to wait.

The next time the doors slid open, I saw Dr. Schoolcraft in full scrubs walking across the corridor with his hands up. Brian walked out of the doors smiling at us, looking very enthusiastic.

"Wow! That was awesome. That was really fast."

A wave of sickness washed over me, and I could tell from the look on Dirk's face he was feeling the same way. I knew this was not Brian's fault, so I did my best to contain myself.

"What? They're done?"

Dirk stood up out of his seat. "They already did the transfer?"

There were two other couples in the waiting area with us, but I didn't care. Our nurse knew full well of our plans to be present for the transfer. I couldn't help but give her a tongue lashing when she finally appeared. She looked at me with steely reserve.

"Please calm down."

Apparently, our nurse hadn't received the memo about what happens when you tell an irate, infertile woman who had just traveled 1,200 miles to watch her surrogate's embryo transfer to calm down. Her words just made me see red and to be honest, I have no idea what exactly I said to her. Her supervisor was not any more empathetic and escalated the situation by asking me to lower my voice. I didn't know how to communicate to either one of these women that this moment, for which we had traveled a long distance so we could be present, was so special to us, and was taken from us.

A few minutes later Dr. Schoolcraft came to speak with us and tried to comfort us by telling us it had been a quick two-minute procedure and that we hadn't missed out on much. Dirk measured his words carefully as he spoke to Dr. Schoolcraft.

"I don't know if you're a spiritual man, but prayer has brought us here. It may have been only two minutes, but what was taken away from us was one hundred percent of that experience. We wanted to pray over our embryos and over Tiffany, and that opportunity was stolen from us. We wanted to take photos of the embryos while they were up on the screen. Since Steph can't carry them, being in the room when our babies would be transferred into Tiffany was everything." Honestly, I wasn't sure if Dr. Schoolcraft would understand how we were feeling. He was a man of science, after all. I was actually a bit surprised to hear how heartfelt his apology was.

"I'm so sorry. I get it. I am a spiritual man too."

As we left the hospital, I knew I had to find a way to pull myself up by the bootstraps. I didn't want this screwup to create a cloud over the experience. After Tiffany was released, we all climbed into the car and drove back to the hotel. We took advantage of the four of us being together in the car and said a prayer before getting out.

Brian led us and asked God to give us a miracle. Each of us took a turn. Tiffany prayed for "God's Best" and also that the baby or babies would be perfectly placed in the womb. I loved the term "God's Best" and started incorporating it in my prayers too.

That night, we got a call from Dr. Schoolcraft on my cell phone. He apologized and said he felt terrible about what had happened. He sounded sincere, and I greatly appreciated hearing from him. He offered to refund us the amount of our airline tickets but instead, I asked him to donate to our local homeless shelter for high school students. We were touched by his generosity.

Dirk and I both believed that we had the luck of the Irish (sometimes lucky and sometimes unlucky). Therefore, when negative things happen, we just want to make sure that everyone learns from those mistakes or opportunities to make things better the next time.

The next day, my mother escorted Aidan to the gate at the airport back home. He boarded a plane to fly out all by himself to meet us for the weekend. Although he was only seven, he had flown many times with us, so it was an old hat to him. We met him at the airport gate as soon as he got off the plane in Colorado.

He still had no idea what was going on. We had flown him out in the guise of taking him skiing, and had told him that we had a friend we wanted him to meet. When we arrived at the hotel, Tiffany was lying in bed. As Aidan shook her hand, I couldn't help but think that his brother and/or sister was inside of Tiffany and that he could be a big brother in a matter of months.

Before packing up and heading up to the mountains, we prayed over Tiffany. It was only about a ninety-minute drive to Breckenridge. I was looking forward to the crisp air and beautiful mountains. We had no more gotten out of Denver when I started coughing. After about an hour, I felt exhausted.

By the time we arrived in Breckenridge, I felt like I had pneumonia or flu. My lungs burned and I could barely keep my eyes open. Dirk took me straight to the ski clinic, which was full of people with broken bones. The thin air made it even more difficult for me to breathe. A triage nurse gave me a mask to wear in the waiting room. Two hours later I was diagnosed with a bad case of the flu. On the way back to our hotel, we stopped at the grocery store for Tamiflu and groceries. I felt awful.

Four days later I was still in bed. I hadn't been outside, much less had any fresh air. Dirk's brother Scott and his wife, who lived in Denver, drove up for a visit and we Facetimed my mother-in-law. I told her all about our disappointment on the day of the transfer and how mad I still was.

"Well, you know why you weren't supposed to be in the room for the transfer? God was protecting you, Tiffany, and those babies."

The hair on my arms stood straight up. She was absolutely right. Had I been in the room, I might have compromised the health of our embryos. I was suddenly so grateful for the misunderstanding that had prevented me from being present for the transfer.

Two weeks later Tiffany went in for a pregnancy blood test, and we were on pins and needles while we awaited the result. We were super nervous, but so excited. Dirk came home early from work so we could take the call from CCRM together. I heard myself squealing as the nurse delivered the positive results of the blood test to us.

"Congratulations! You all are pregnant."

There were no words to express our joy. There was no way to describe it. We were overwhelmed with gratitude as we called our families and Stacy and Rennie to share our glorious news—we were pregnant.

CHAPTER 36

Sacred Ground

Two weeks later we drove to Dallas for our first ultrasound with Tiffany. The appointment was bright and early, so we left our home just as the sun was rising. I could feel my heart racing as we pulled out of the driveway. Dirk, of course, was calm as can be. You never would have known it was the day we were finding out if we were having one baby or two, and potentially what their sexes were.

The long drive was our first opportunity to openly discuss this major secret, which we had been keeping from Aidan. He didn't know anything yet, so up until now we had been very cautious around him. Now that we were alone, I could finally take Dirk through all of the "what ifs."

"What if there are two heartbeats?"

Like the lawyer he was, Dirk tossed the question right back at me with a grin on his face.

"What if?"

I couldn't help giggling at the thought of finally bringing Aidan's baby furniture out of storage and the possibility of doing some shopping for not just one baby but two. Of course, I was also aware that like our friends who had twins, we would probably disappear for at least three years. Still, I was giddy at the thought.

It was hard to believe we had already arrived at this place in our journey. As we coasted through the Arbuckle Mountains, I thought about the enormity of what we had been through and everything that had brought us to this sacred time.

Our journey was not unlike that of the engineers who had used dynamite to blast their way through the granite rocks to build the highway we were on. Instead of explosives, Dirk and I had forged our path with our faith, perseverance, and the medical science made available to us by God.

We were no strangers to the drive to Dallas, since my sister lived there with her husband and two little boys. We knew that as soon as we crossed the Red River into Texas, the speed limit would drop by ten miles an hour. By the time we reached the border, my adrenaline was pounding. It had been six long years, but now everything was moving fast, so I welcomed the opportunity to slow down the car and my mind.

There wouldn't be time on this trip to visit with my sister and her family, since we were determined to get back home to Aidan. Melanie had just shared that she was pregnant with her third child. For the last four years she had been either pregnant or breastfeeding while I struggled with my infertility. I was a bit envious. I realized this was my own struggle, but I couldn't help comparing myself to her. I prayed for God to bind up these feelings and to help me feel nothing but joy when it came to Tiffany as well. I didn't know if I would feel envious of her.

Tiffany was outside the hospital waiting for us when we arrived. I could tell she was knee deep in first trimester sickness. I was so anxious to get the ultrasound started. A technician called the three of us back. The stares that we got from people as we walked past them in the waiting room were comical to me. I almost turned and whispered "we are sister wives" to the pregnant women, but nerves got the best of me.

Before we began the ultrasound, we had a quick prayer.

"Lord, we thank you for the blessing of Tiffany and the miracle of this pregnancy. We submit and trust you. Whether it's one or two heartbeats, let the baby look beautiful," I said.

I was on the edge of my seat as the technician captured images of Tiffany's uterus.

"Okay, I see a heartbeat. It is good and strong."

"Oh . . . I see another heartbeat! Congratulations—you have twins!"

The technician had barely finished her sentence when I heard myself screaming.

"Oh my gosh, oh my gosh. Thank you, God. Thank you, God."

I looked at the screen and there they were—two miracles. I couldn't help but sob. I was so emotional I thought I might pass out. I had to sit down.

I looked over at Dirk and saw tears streaming down his face. He was beaming. It was the most beautiful smile—one that I had been wanting to see from him for six years. We looked over at Tiffany and she was crying too. I ran over to her and hugged her and kissed her on the cheek.

"Tiffany, I don't know what else to say but thank you!"

We both laughed and cried, and then I had to sit down again. The technician smiled at all three of us.

"Your babies look beautiful. We will see you in one month for another ultrasound."

By the time Dr. Roberts came into the room, I was doing full-on Lamaze breathing to keep myself calm. He was very nice with a polite bedside manner; meeting him put us at ease. Even though he was very likable and made sure to treat all three of us like we were the patient, my emotions were running high. I was squeezing Dirk's hand so hard, I actually hurt him.

"Steph, please let go."

Ever his folksy self, Dirk couldn't help but ask the doctor where he was from. My jaw just about dropped at Dr. Roberts's response. Not only was he from Oklahoma—Dr. Roberts also happened to be from the same little university town where we lived. In fact, he had gone to the same elementary school where Aidan was sitting at this very moment. What were the odds?

I knew then that God was tying us all together. I felt super connected to Dr. Roberts and comfortable with him. I also recognized that the "coincidence" was an affirmation that we were exactly where we were supposed to be.

We knew we weren't out the woods, but with Tiffany's history and all of the positive signs from God, we knew it was time to tell Aidan. I had bought a few books on surrogacy to help him understand, but we weren't exactly sure of what we were going to say. The truth was, I was nervous to tell him.

I still remembered my parents telling me that I was going to be a big sister at the age of five. I was so scared that I refused to come out of my closet for hours. I was so worried about who would take care of me once my sister had arrived. I knew I didn't want us to make Aidan feel that way.

On the way back home, we stopped to buy a twin picture frame and put the ultrasound pictures on each side. Thanks to genetic testing, we would know the sex of the babies that afternoon at four o'clock! Once we had heard from CCRM, it would be time to let Aidan know that God had heard his prayers.

I was on pins and needles when Katie, our nurse at CCRM, called on my cell phone. Dirk and I were in our master bedroom. My palms were sweaty and my heart was racing practically out of my chest. This was it.

This was the moment we had been waiting for.

Not just for the last couple of months. This was the moment we had been waiting for—for so many years.

"Stephanie, this is Katie with CCRM! Congratulations to you, Dirk, and Tiffany. We got all your results and the babies look beautiful. So, let's get to it. Are you ready to know the sex of your babies?"

My mind immediately began to wander. Did she say sex of my

babies? Does that mean they are the same sex?

"Yes!" I screamed and sat on the bed. Then I stood right back up.

"Okay, embryo 4AB is . . . a boy!"

Her voice went up at the end of the word "boy." I thought I knew what that meant. I couldn't help but wonder to myself, if it were two boys, wouldn't she have just said so?

I was so thrilled to have another boy. Aidan and I had such a special bond . . . and boys truly love their mommies. I thought of stinky, dirty little feet and cried. I forgot to even look at Dirk for his reaction because I was anticipating what I would hear next.

As Katie continued, there was something in the inflection of her voice that told me God knew my heart's desires.

"And embryo 4BB is . . . a girl."

I screamed when I heard the beginning of that magical word, and then I burst into tears and started sobbing. I looked over at Dirk and saw that he was grinning from ear to ear. Dirk and I hugged. I thanked Katie over and over again.

"Oh my gosh! Oh my gosh!"

"I get to go to the Daddy-Daughter Dance!" Dirk exclaimed.

It was perfect. One of each. We got to experience having a boy all over again and we were going to have a daughter! A girl. I couldn't believe it. It took me an hour or so to come down off of my high. We couldn't wait to tell Aidan.

A little while later we brought Aidan home from my parents' house and sat him down on the couch.

"Aidan, we've got exciting news."

His big blue eyes lit up.

"What have you been praying for?"

He furrowed his full eyebrows and gave it some thought.

"A brother or a sister?"

"Yes! Well, we have some exciting news. God has answered your prayers! You are going to be a big brother."

Aidan was so excited, he gasped. And just when I thought I couldn't get any more emotional, my little boy got up and hugged me, then hugged Dirk. Feelings welled up inside me as I handed him his frame and watched him open it up.

"And we have more news! We're having twins! You're getting a brother *and* a sister."

Aidan gasped again. "I'm going to be a big brother." He beamed, stood up, and did a little dance.

"Yes!"

It just about killed me when he ran over to me, bent forward, and kissed my belly. I knew then that I couldn't tell him in stages. I couldn't lie to him. I had to explain it all to him now—the whole shebang.

We sat him back down and waited for a few minutes for the news to soak in.

Then we braced ourselves for the rest of the conversation. "This might be confusing for you, but the babies are not in my belly. You see, Mommy's tummy is broken. Mommy has been to lots of doctors and we felt like it was best for someone else to carry our babies."

It felt so cathartic to finally say the words and tell Aidan the truth. All these years, we had done everything we could to protect him from feelings of sadness or loss. It broke my heart to see tears streaming down his face.

"What does that mean?"

"I can't carry babies. My tummy is broken. So the doctor took cells from Mommy and from Daddy and created embryos. They were put into someone else's tummy. We are borrowing a pouch, like a kangaroo."

Aidan's face was so sad.

"That's weird."

I was in absolute anguish watching him. Dirk tried to encourage him.

"It's awesome, son!" Dirk said.

"It is weird, Aidan, because it's not what we're used to. I know this is a lot to take in. Do you remember meeting Tiffany in Colorado? We are borrowing her pouch. She is pregnant for us," I told him.

Aidan started to cry in a high-pitched way. Dirk grabbed him and put his arms around him.

"It's okay buddy. Come here!"

The cadence of Aidan's voice broke down into a painful, halting pattern.

"I— don't—understand. How did they transport your baby in her?"

I did my best to sound cheerful. "Through an operation. Tiffany is an angel to us. We're very lucky to have her."

I grabbed him and wrapped him up in my arms. "Once the babies are born, they're ours forever. Aidan, your prayers worked! You asked for a brother and a sister and God answered your prayers! You are going to be a big brother!"

Aidan sniffled for a few minutes. We hugged and kissed him. He looked down at the picture of the ultrasounds and smiled. Then like the typical seven-year-old boy he was, he got over it and asked if could run outside to play.

CHAPTER 37

Sister Wives

My mom came to Dallas with Dirk and me for the very next appointment. She had never met Tiffany and wanted to meet the woman who was carrying her grandchildren. My mom smiled with her whole face when she saw Tiffany for the first time.

"It's so nice to meet you. Thank you so much. You're such a blessing . . . We'll never be able to thank you enough."

I saw my mom pause. I knew it was because she wanted to hug her. Tiffany was very sweet and welcomed my mom's warm embrace. Then I paused when I saw my mom reach out and place her hand on Tiffany's belly.

Honestly, I hadn't thought about it until now and wasn't sure what was appropriate. I felt the need to jump in and bring a little humor to the situation.

"Well Tiffany, talking about getting to know you up close and personal. How about someone you just met touching your belly?" Tiffany gave us both a big smile and laughed.

"Oh, it's okay."

I couldn't help breaking into a sarcastic verse of "Getting to Know You" from *The Sound of Music*. We all laughed because it was sooooo awkward, but wildly wonderful as well.

In the waiting room, we got the usual stares. We must have been such a sight—Dirk with a small harem of women. We had a different technician from the last time and I could tell she was surprised. Once we were in the room, I set the record straight. The last thing I wanted was for the technician to think my mom, Tiffany, and I were all sister wives.

"We're the parents and Tiffany is our gestational carrier."

The technician was so touched. She stared at Tiffany in awe.

"Oh my gosh! That is amazing!"

My mom was usually a talker, but the sound of her twin grandchildren's heartbeats left her speechless. The technician looked over at me as she carefully moved the probe.

"The babies' heartbeats sound beautiful."

I couldn't have agreed with her more. I squeezed Dirk's hand as we listened to the rapidly pulsing heartbeats of our twins.

Once my mom recovered from the disbelief of hearing and seeing the babies, she was back to being herself. God bless her, she launched into a five-minute story about her pregnancy with me—and even inserted the story about the congenital dislocation of the hip I was born with. I finally had to interrupt her so Tiffany could get up off the table.

Over the next eight months, we had at least a dozen OB appointments in Dallas with Tiffany. Some weeks we stayed overnight with my sister and her family. It was a very sweet and special time. My sister's baby bump was now visible.

Another part of our routine were the stares we got in the waiting room. It was even funnier when my in-laws came to one of the early ultrasounds. Now there were two O'Hara men and three of us women.

Once again it was a new technician, so I was compelled to explain that Dirk and I were the parents and Tiffany was our carrier—a modern family if you will.

It was so special to watch Forrest and Loretta's expressions as the ultrasound got under way. Loretta's eyes filled with tears as the 4D images of the babies' faces came to life on the screen. The technician smiled as she studied the moving image.

"The babies look beautiful."

Normally a man of few words, my father-in-law was particularly expressive toward Tiffany.

"Well, what you're doing is very special. Thank you for doing this. They waited a long time."

As magical as it was sharing the ultrasounds with our families, it was a bit awkward. Tiffany was amazing. Even though she was exposing her ever-expanding stomach to people she had just met, she embraced the experience.

I had no idea what to expect when I brought my father along, since he was always the wild card. I never knew what was going to come out of his mouth. This time, instead of being stunned, I was touched by the poignancy of his words to Tiffany.

"Uh, Tiffany, uh, you're such a blessing to our family. You'll have many jewels in your heavenly crown for your good deeds."

My dad definitely had a sweet side. As soon as he met Tiffany he had an immediate affinity for her, just the way he did for Stacy and all of my other close friends. He thought of them all as his daughters. I could tell Tiffany understood how heartfelt my father's sentiments were.

"Thank you. It is my pleasure."

Because she was carrying twins, Tiffany was considered high risk. Since she was in this category, we were also monitored by two specialists. One of them was Dr. Abassi, a young French doctor who was very caring, and her two partners. At every visit, they used the same word—beautiful—to describe every aspect of our babies. Their appearance, the sound of their heartbeats, the amount of fluid, even their placement was described with that one glorious word—beautiful. I couldn't hear this word enough. After so many horrific ultrasounds, I could have bathed in the word.

The word also echoed Tiffany's petition to God on the day of the transfer. She had asked God for his best. I had asked that "the baby, whether there was one or two, look beautiful." I had held on to that phrase and at every visit, our prayer was affirmed. This was a powerful lesson for me. Through these words, the Lord really impressed upon me that all those years we weren't receiving was because we were willing to settle. He wanted to give us the desires of our hearts, but we were in a dark place, willing to accept mediocrity.

It was only when I was finally sick and tired of being sick and tired that Dirk and I started aiming our sights higher. We had been so bogged down by fear, and our expectations were set so low, that God couldn't send us his best or his beautiful. When we were finally done with failure and sought with our entire hearts—our entire beings—God revealed His plan to us.

At the end of Tiffany's first trimester, CCRM called to release all four of us from their care. I was very excited, but at a loss for words. I didn't know what to say to the doctor and the nurse who had assisted in our miracle.

Before this day arrived, Dirk and I had agreed that anytime anybody asked about the babies, we would give all glory and praise to God. He had worked all things together for our good the way it is written in Romans 8:28—"And we know that all things work together for good to them that love God, to them that are called according to his purpose." He had not just restored us, but instead had rewarded us with double as much, as promised in Isaiah 61:7—"Instead of your shame you will receive a double portion, and instead of disgrace you will rejoice in your inheritance. And so you will inherit a double portion in your land, and everlasting joy will be yours."

CHAPTER 38

Moscow Mule

I was still in complete shock about having twins when I saw my friend Apryl. She lived down the street from my parents and had her own boy/girl twins around the same age as Aidan. Aidan loved her son and often had playdates with him.

One evening, when I stopped by to pick up Aidan from their home, I asked Apryl to give me the skinny on what it was actually like to have twins. We hadn't gone public with our news yet so I was very careful not to give anything away. I just couldn't stop myself from staring at her twins, Aly and Kane.

Apryl was a spunky, very well put together blonde who loved to entertain. So of course, when I showed up she offered to mix up her favorite cocktail—a Moscow Mule. After taking a couple of sips, I discreetly asked about what it was like when Aly and Kane were newborns. Apryl laughed as recalled that time.

"It was hard in the second month when both babies were up in the middle of the night screaming."

Before she could say much more, Apryl's husband Brandon came into the room. Brandon was the kind of guy who had never known a stranger in his whole life. When I asked him about parenting infant twins, he did not hold back.

"It was *insane*! We got no sleep! We were up four, five, six times a night!" Brandon's words reverberated through the room. "We already had Reese, who was two," he continued. "I remember one time when it was three in the morning. Both Kane and Aly were up—crying that newborn cry. They wouldn't stop! We were so tired. Apryl and I just looked at each other and started laughing."

Apryl smiled and nodded in agreement with her husband.

"You're either going to laugh or cry."

I took another sip of my vodka-infused cocktail. After hearing their tales from the trenches, I kind of wanted to cry.

My mind was racing during the two-minute drive home. When I walked in the door, Dirk was there. I told him about the conversation with Apryl and Brandon. We both giggled and thought, "Eh." We would gladly welcome and embrace newborn twins waking up in the middle of the night!

This was the week we had planned to announce our big secret on Facebook. I had known for a while exactly how I wanted to share our news. There were a lot of topics to address in one post, so it had to be done very thoughtfully. I knew it was crucial for me to address the fact that I wasn't pregnant. A girlfriend of mine was a photographer, so I called her up and she came right over.

Aidan and his persistent—not to mention bold—prayers had served as a powerful catalyst in our journey, so I wanted him to be front and center in our announcement. Fortunately for me, my son was not at all camera shy. I made a cross for him to hold that said, "For this child, I have prayed." Next to that was a sign that said, "O'Hara Twins Coming Fall 2015." Then we had five pairs of shoes lined up, starting with Dirk's, then mine, Aidan's, and a darling little pair of pink shoes and a pair of blue shoes. It only took us about half an hour to get the shots. With each picture we took, it became more difficult to contain my excitement.

The photographs of Aidan were emailed to me that same night. I chose three to upload in our post. I took a deep breath and shook off the nervous energy as I sat down to type our news in the most honest and simplistic terms:

We have exciting news! We are expecting twins—a boy and a girl. As many of you know and as we told Aidan, my tummy is broken. An angel is carrying our biological children for us. We are so thankful for this precious gift she is giving to us. God is so good!

I was terrified. For the first time I was telling a thousand of my "friends" that I was infertile; that I had miscarried and that I couldn't carry my own children. We were sharing the news because we wanted people to share in our joy. As we always did, we also wanted to ask for prayer for ourselves, Tiffany, and our unborn children.

I knew I might be judged. I also worried that people would gossip about us. At the end of the day this was our truth, so I just prayed that our community, friends, and family would be accepting of our news.

"Here it goes," I thought to myself as I took a deep breath and hit "post" on the screen. My palms were sweating. It felt so good to go public with the news, but also every bit as terrifying.

I had already decided I wouldn't log on to Facebook until after I had put Aidan to bed that night, but within minutes, my phone was blowing up. I was inundated with phone call after phone call, text messages, and Facebook instant messages. Friends from all walks of life were kind beyond expectations. I was so relieved and grateful.

I had prepared myself for every possible question anyone might ask or anything someone might say. After we posted our news on Facebook, we heard from the mother of one of our friends from Western Oklahoma. She had the sweetest voice and a long, drawn-out accent typical of the area where she lived. She sounded genuinely happy for us as she spoke.

"Stephanie, this is soooooooooo neeeeeeeeeat. It's like you just went over to the TG&Y and picked your babies off the shelf! It's going to be so easy."

I just kind of laughed. God bless her, she really didn't understand what we had been through for the last six years. I knew she had the best of intentions, so I happily accepted her good wishes without giving her the recap of the mountains we had climbed to get here.

One afternoon when I was at our local wine shop buying a bottle of champs (of course), the owner, Kathy, offered her congratulations with a big smile on her face.

"Stephanie, when are those babies coming?"

I clearly wasn't carrying twins, so I felt compelled to explain to those standing behind me in line.

"Oh, I'm not actually pregnant. Someone else is carrying our babies for us you see . . ."

When I was done at the register, one of the managers carried my bag out to my car. He was in his fifties and always eager to help his customers. We always had a friendly conversation whenever he helped me out to the car. Today I could see that he was genuinely excited for us.

"So Stephanie, are y'all adopting?"

I quickly assessed the best way to give him an overview of our long story, considering we were in a liquor store parking lot. I decided to be straightforward.

"Well, no. Someone else is carrying our biological children for us. I can't keep pregnancies."

"Oh, I am sorry! How many did you lose?"

I was a little taken aback by his question, but I could tell he had good intentions. "We lost seven."

"Man! That's awful." Awkward silence followed. "But—I bet you had fun trying to make 'em!"

God bless him. I left that one right where it was standing.

"That's one way of looking at it."

Even my own father was confused. This surrogacy business was really throwing him for a loop. As Tiffany edged closer to thirty weeks, my dad and I had the funniest conversation over lunch.

"Now, Stephie, I'm sorry. I don't understand. What happens if these babies come out looking like Tiffany?"

It was hard for me not to laugh.

"Oh, Chuckles, do we need to revisit a biology book?"

"I just don't understand. I mean, Tiffany is beautiful, but what are you going to do if they don't look like you? What if they look like her?"

"Dad, that isn't possible." I went into the same exact elementary explanation as I had with Aidan. They took a cell from my body and one from Dirk's and fertilized the egg with the sperm.

As prepared as I was to answer any question, I could not believe I was having a "birds and bees" conversation with my seventy-year-old father.

Through it all, my communications with Tiffany were the easiest and the best they could have possibly been. We were in touch several times a week by text and email: "Babies and I are doing great! I craved a little chocolate last night and Baby A kicked around afterward. I guess she liked it!"

At her last appointment, we were officially out of the woods. Thirty-six and a half weeks was considered full term with twins, and we were at thirty-one weeks. We knew that even if the babies were delivered early, their chances of survival were very good. Once again, the specialist described the ultrasound as "beautiful." Their heartbeats were strong and fast, and their measurements were perfect.

Dr. Roberts was mildly concerned about Tiffany's blood pressure, which was high at times. He advised us that if Tiffany's blood pressure escalated, she would have to go to the emergency room and deliver by C-section. Dirk and I were of course a bit concerned about the logistics of getting to Dallas in time for the delivery, but we weren't worried. Truthfully, I was more worried about my sister, who was so hormonal and emotional. Poor thing was expending a lot of her mental energy coordinating which delivery room our parents should go to in the unlikely event that she and Tiffany went into labor at the same time.

We felt protected by God and knew that everything would be okay. We knew in our hearts everything would unfold just as it was supposed to.

CHAPTER 39

You Prayed for This

After so many years of being on an emotional roller coaster, the summer truly felt like one long soiree. There was so much joy around us and so much to celebrate! In addition to welcoming our twins and my sister's baby, we were also planning a big weekend affair to celebrate my parents' fiftieth wedding anniversary.

We had two parties planned for my parents. The second was a more formal party at our golf club, where my band played. The first bash was a small catered party at their home for family. I could already see my mom, with her wedding scrapbook on her lap, going through the story behind every last receipt from their wedding day and honeymoon night at the Howard Johnson's.

With family and friends coming from all over the country to celebrate their golden wedding anniversary, it also seemed like the perfect time for my baby shower. When my sister Melanie, Apryl, Stacy, and Melissa offered to throw one for me, my mind immediately went to that weekend. I knew it would be hectic, but it was also a unique chance to include childhood friends as well as my family, who we didn't get to see as often as we would have liked. After some discussion with Dirk and my sister, I decided to go big. After all, I knew that once the babies arrived, Dirk and I would be forced into hiding with parental duties.

True to Melanie's typical form, she chose royalty as the theme for my shower. It was all pomp and circumstance inside Apryl's house, which was decorated with darling prince and princess party favors, hanging banners, and centerpieces. Family and friends from all walks of life literally arrived to the royal fanfare of a cute junior high trumpet player Melanie had hired for the afternoon. He was wearing a long white dress shirt with black pants and played his little heart out.

I had been looking forward to this shower for years and years. I looked around the room at the faces of so many people I loved and basked in it. I felt so blessed and grateful, I almost didn't believe it was real. I was so moved I couldn't let the night go by without thanking everyone and of course, I cried as I spoke.

I first thanked them for being on the roller coaster with me the last six years and told them how much their friendships meant to me. I thanked Mel and Apryl for throwing such a beautiful shower and told them that I had dreamt about this day for a long time. As I chugged the last of the champs in my glass, I joked, "So once the babies come, I will see you all in about three years when I come up for air—right, Apryl?"

Even though I had no clue what I was in for with newborn twins, I did know that I needed to make hay while the sun shined with my best girls. After the shower, I rounded up about fifteen of my girlfriends and off we went to Opie's, a hole-in-the-wall bar with a great dance floor. It wasn't much to look at from the outside but inside, with its shag carpet, disco balls, and tables at the edge of the dance floor, it was like something out of Studio 54.

My very best friend from childhood, Sherry, had flown into town from Atlanta. We broke out our high school dance moves to Bobby Brown's "My Prerogative." We danced and laughed all night. It felt so good to let loose with the girls. They were my angels and helped me to celebrate one of the most special nights of my life.

During all of the ups and downs over the last six years, friends from Bible study had also been supportive and encouraging. My friend Kathleen in particular never gave up hope. Originally from Texas, Kathleen had big, sweet brown eyes and thick, long blonde hair. She was soft-spoken and had a southern drawl.

"I just know that you're going to get pregnant and I am going to throw you the biggest and best baby shower" she had said to me during my dark times, with tears welling up in her eyes.

It was that kind of generosity of spirit that helped get me through days when I was running low on hope. She was truly the kind of friend who would help lift me up when my wings had forgotten how to fly. I was so thankful for Kathleen's friendship. We had so much fun together, going on girls' trips to Colorado and Mexico amongst other places. We were also connected by our faith, praying for each other and truly wanting the best for each other.

Kathleen made good on her promise, and she and her husband threw a couples' shower for Dirk and me at their beautiful home. Several of our couples friends from church also co-hosted. It was an outdoor party in Kathleen's backyard, complete with a gorgeous tent. Appropriately, the theme was "The O'Hara Band is Growing," so there was an acoustic duo playing.

It felt so special to be showered with love by these people who knew everything we had been through as a couple. Many of them had even been in the room on the day I miscarried in church. They had prayed for us, sent us thoughtful gifts, and now were celebrating God's goodness with us.

Our guests wrote hilarious messages on newborn diapers. The idea was for us to read them when we were in the middle of a diaper change at three in the morning. Dirk and I cracked up as we read them out loud. The messages ranged from a heartfelt "So much to be thankful for" to the literal "Shit happens," and of course the ironic "You prayed for this."

CHAPTER 40

Circle of Life

At the end of the summer we were once again confronted with the circle of life when my mom's brother, Johnny Smith, died. We knew something was wrong when he didn't come down for the anniversary party, but his death was still a shock. He was my mom's only sibling. I always remembered his deep voice, unmistakable whistle, and his golf-course-perfect lawn. He was a man who loved his wife and his daughters deeply, and his love extended to his dogs as well.

His passing was very emotional for my mom for many reasons. Amongst them was that he was the last living member of her immediate family, the Smiths. Fifty years ago, she had become a Cotton when she married my dad. Now, all of the Smiths with the exception of Johnny's wife, my Aunt Jeanne, were gone.

After my uncle's funeral, my mom and I went up to clean out Gigi's house so it could be put up for sale. A flood of memories channeled through me as soon as we walked through the door. The smell of the house, the linoleum floor print, and the texture of Gigi's old couch she called the "divan" triggered powerful memories for both me and my mom.

My grandparents had survived the Great Depression and managed to buy their house in 1959. For fifty years the Smiths had called it home. In so many ways, this was the house that had shaped my mom and forged her future. Gigi had been an integral part of raising me and had a profound influence on my faith. I was so grateful she had lived long enough to meet Aidan and my sister's firstborn son, Tripp.

It took a week or so to clean out the house. After all was said and done, we were exhausted and emotionally spent. As we put the last of the boxes in the car, I noticed the wrought iron plaque ornament on the front door. It was an ornate "S," for Smith. I looked over at my mom, who was loading some boxes into her SUV.

"Can I have this off the door?"

My mom looked at me and paused.

"Sure!"

I got the screwdriver out of her toolbox. Taking the plaque off the door had an overwhelming sense of finality. As I carefully wrapped it up and placed it in the car, I felt grateful to have this little piece of family history that I could hold on to.

CHAPTER 41

The Time Capsule

By the end of the summer, we had narrowed down the list of possible names for our babies to a dozen. We had a combination of family names, Celtic names, and some modern ones, too. Aidan, who was a big fan of the Oklahoma City Thunder basketball team, thoughtfully suggested Russell for his baby brother and "KayDee" for his baby sister. My top pick was Arden for a girl, and I loved Finn for a boy. And just when I thought I had sold Dirk on the unique Irish boy's name, we met three little boys named Finn in one day and I promptly had to cross it off the list.

We talked about baby names on our long car rides to Dallas for our doctor appointments with Tiffany. Just as we had with Aidan's name, we wanted their names to have significance. When Aidan was born, his name paid homage to both my father-in-law's family as well as my mother-in-law's family. We now wanted to pay tribute to my mom, especially given the circumstance that her younger brother had just passed away. She brought over the thick genealogy books Gigi had researched and compiled over the years, but never made any suggestions for names. My dad, on the other hand, had his own short list: Kathryn for his mother, and Estelle for his grandmother; Braxton and William for his uncle and cousin. Some of these he had suggested when Aidan was born.

Dirk's parents didn't really have the kind of details that Gigi had uncovered at libraries and city halls all over the state. We did have his family tree and were able to look back at three generations of his family. Some of the names, like Edna Earl and Nell Ruth, were quite southern.

My father-in-law had fond memories of his Aunt Stella, whom he remembered as a little spry lady, full of spunk, but we couldn't make any decisions because we wanted two names that sounded cute together.

At the rate of our progress, I was a little worried Tiffany would go into labor before we could narrow our list down further. We were in touch with her a couple of times a week through texts and emails. She was amazing about communicating all the pregnancy milestones she was experiencing. There was one perinatal appointment we had to miss because we were traveling, so she sent me an email with wonderful details:

Babies both looked great! Baby girl (a) still head down, very active, and 1 lb 13oz. 145 heartbeat. Measures 25 weeks 4 days. She wasn't taking good pics today . . . couldn't get her face. Baby boy (b) is now head down, had hiccups, and 2 lbs. 141 heart beat. Measures 26 weeks 2 days. She said hearts, brains, bones, fluids and all body parts looked beautiful . . .

Every day we took steps toward preparing for the arrival of our twins. I didn't take any of it for granted. Whether it was painting their nursery with our Godsons, ordering the rocker, or packing Aidan's emergency bag, since he was going to miss some school—even the most mundane tasks were revelatory.

It had been six years since I had gone to the storage facility where we had stored all of Aidan's baby clothes, toys, and nursery items like his bassinet. All these years, it was Dirk who went by every couple of months to take everything from Aidan's GAP onesies to the beloved John Deere boots he had outgrown. For six years, we had stored these things away not knowing if we would ever use them again. In the time that had passed, my sister had had two children, but as weird as it sounds, we didn't want to jinx anything by passing Aidan's things along.

Today, Dirk and I had come to the storage facility together for the first time. I was taken aback by the flood of emotion I felt when I walked in. It was like walking into a time capsule. I had a mental tally of everything we had packed up for storage, but I hadn't seen any of it in ages. I couldn't believe how much time had passed so quickly—Aidan was about to start the second grade.

There were rows and rows of plastic storage boxes all labeled with different milestones from the first six years of Aidan's life. There were also board books and his collection of Matchbox cars, and I gushed when I saw his John Deere pedal tractor. My heart was bursting when I found his darling Curious George pajamas. It seemed impossible that he had ever been small enough to fit into them. I was just as incredulous that in just a few weeks' time, there would be babies in these clothes again. I held up the pajamas so Dirk could see them.

"Honey, I just can't believe we get to use these again!"

Dirk paused.

"You know—I had to bring load after load here for six years. I didn't look forward to coming here."

His tone made me stop what I was doing. He was uncharacteristically emotional, which I didn't see very often. I put my arms around him. It suddenly occurred to me that all these years he didn't feel like there was room for his emotions. I had endured the physical part and found ways to express my grief, never thinking how hard this was on him, too.

We held one another for a long time. I thought about how much we had grown since the day he proposed—both as individuals and as a couple. Six years ago, we had embarked on this infertility journey together and come out stronger. I was so thankful we had learned so much about one another, our marriage, and faith.

Together we had learned that things don't always turn out perfectly or in the time we would like. Instead of turning our backs on God, we had submitted to God and His plan. As difficult as that had been, it had enriched our relationship and created a bond between us to the point that no matter what life might throw at us, it would only strengthen us.

CHAPTER 42

Second Rodeo

In the last few weeks of her pregnancy, Tiffany's baby belly jutted straight out. I imagined she must be so uncomfortable, but true to her incredible attitude, she never said a thing. We were in planning stages now that included submitting all sorts of legal, financial, and insurance paperwork to the hospital. The time had also come for us to take a tour of the hospital, which Dirk and I decided to do after one of Tiffany's perinatal appointments.

The hospital tour was a completely different experience this time around. I thought back to when I was pregnant with Aidan. We had taken every kind of class the hospital had offered—Lamaze, baby care, and breastfeeding, as well as labor and delivery. I remembered showing up to the hospital tour with a thick binder full of questions, all of which were answered that afternoon.

Just as it had when I was pregnant with Aidan, touring the hospital where our twins would be born made it very real for me. I was happy to learn that the hospital staff was somewhat familiar with the process since they had two surrogate births on record. The hospital administrator said that when the twins came, they would give us a room for Tiffany and an additional room for us and the babies, and not charge for it. Dirk and I appreciated this sensitive gesture so much because it made us feel like we were being treated like any other parents coming to the hospital to have a baby.

I was in less of a nervous state this time around for a couple reasons.

First, I wasn't pregnant. Second, and perhaps more important, this wasn't my first rodeo. I already knew about that sacred bond between parent and child and was excited to experience it for the second and third time. I had an appreciation for all of the emotional rewards of parenting, such as giving your babies their first bath, watching their first smile, and hearing their first "coo."

I was also very familiar with the more grueling aspects of motherhood. I could still remember being sleep deprived and feeling like a zombie. I vividly remembered the challenges of not producing enough milk for Aidan and the stress that it caused both of us.

This time around I wanted to be kind to myself while being the best mommy to my newborn babies and to Aidan. When Aidan was an infant, I would say, "I've got this." It was hard for me to ask for help, and it was difficult for me to accept it. I knew this needed to change. Dirk and I were older now—in our forties—and our parents, who were always happy to jump in and help with Aidan, were now in their seventies.

Over and again, I heard the same sentiment from different girlfriends whom I considered "twin guru moms."

"Don't do this by yourself," said one fellow twin mom. "Don't try to be a hero," said another. And of course, my friend Apryl, who had boy-girl twins, was adamant: "You've got to ask for help."

This time around I was determined to accept offers from friends who wanted to come by and rock the babies or help feed them. I had come to realize that by turning them down as I had in the past, I had denied them an opportunity to bless us. I had heard the phrase "The greatest blessing in the whole world is being a blessing." Tiffany, Brian, Dirk, and I had talked about this at length. Saying "no thank you" to someone who asks if they can help is literally robbing them of an opportunity to bless you.

Dirk and I had a schedule in mind. We knew that if we could each get four hours of straight REM-cycle sleep a couple of nights per week, we would be in good shape. We also knew how unpredictable babies could be, so we decided to hire a night nurse a couple of times a week. It would be another expense, but we knew it would make us better parents to our twins and of course to Aidan, whom we did not want to feel neglected.

When I called our local hospital to see if there might be a nurse who would be interested in helping us, we were told that it wasn't something they could help us with. I then turned to the internet. I figured that since that is where we found Tiffany, we would likely find the perfect person to be our night nurse there too. I posted an ad on a website and waited.

We had numerous qualified applicants, but there was one that gave me that same feeling I had felt when I saw Tiffany's application. Amy was a certified post-partum doula. On the day of her interview, I immediately saw her kind heart and nurturing personality. I knew instantly she was the one.

The only thing we still didn't have a plan for was the birth. We knew Tiffany was going to have a C-section, but we had no way of knowing when she would go into labor. My sister was a little freaked about the possibility that the birth of our twins and her daughter might coincide. She didn't want to miss the birth of our twins, and we didn't want to miss the birth of her daughter. I had to admit, we were cutting it close. But if there was one thing Dirk and I had learned over the years, it was that there were certain things that were completely out of our control. And this was definitely one of them.

CHAPTER 43

LABOR Day Weekend

It was hard to believe the summer was drawing to a close and Aidan was starting the second grade. He was such a handsome kid; tall and skinny, with Dirk's inquisitive mind and wit. As we approached the entrance it suddenly occurred to me this might be the last time I would be able to drop him off at school for a while. I looked at him and got a little choked up. I prayed that he would always feel loved and special to us, no matter how crazy our lives would become.

Tiffany was at week thirty-five of her pregnancy, and it was time for one of her final checkups with Dr. Roberts. Seeing her at the appointment brought to mind my final weeks of pregnancy with Aidan, when I felt excited, nervous, and anxious to meet him.

There was no ultrasound scheduled for today. Instead, Dr. Roberts took measurements of her growing belly. He also checked Tiffany's hands and feet for swelling, which I could see was starting to happen. Based on my own calculations, I thought we would have at least a couple more weeks (which would put us in the middle of September). Tiffany's prediction, based on how she was feeling, was that the babies would come on Labor Day weekend, which was just a few days away.

Dr. Roberts expressed mild concern about Tiffany's blood pressure, which was slightly elevated.

"Worst-case scenario is an emergency C-section. If your pressure rises at all, go straight to the hospital."

Despite his cautionary words, I was as cool as a cucumber. I didn't the let medical possibilities get the best of me like I had years earlier. I had seen the neonatal intensive care unit, and from a medical standpoint I knew our babies had a very high chance of survival even if they were a few weeks premature. On the spiritual side, I had prayed that I would have peace and no anxiety. Unlike years past, I knew that I had to trust that everything would be fine. Dirk and I had handed this to God. We knew He was in control, and we found comfort in that.

My sister was set to be induced on the Tuesday after Labor Day at a hospital just a few miles away from where Tiffany would deliver our twins. As it came down to the wire, she continued to worry about Tiffany going into labor on the same day as her induction. For the last few weeks, we seemed to have the same conversation.

"Steph, we need to have a plan!"

"No, we don't, Mel. Everything will work out."

I realized I was much more relaxed than she was because I wasn't pregnant. I also knew that the chances of Tiffany going into labor while Melanie was in labor were miniscule. As the long weekend rolled in, I felt that there was nothing to worry about.

It was a typical Labor Day weekend for us. We had company in town and went to the OU football game. We relaxed with Stacy and Rennie and Melissa and Ben. All weekend I kept my phone nearby and checked for texts or missed calls from Tiffany. It seemed the babies were also taking the weekend to relax.

On Monday night we put Aidan to bed. As we always did, we prayed for our twins and for Tiffany. Once Aidan was asleep, I went into the family room and got to work changing photos into some new frames I had bought. As I was sitting on the couch taping a photo into a frame, Dirk walked in.

"I just spoke to Tiffany. Her blood pressure is 165/120. She's headed to the hospital."

Dirk's words caught me completely off guard. I sat straight up and could feel my own blood pressure start to elevate. It was go time!

Without skipping a beat, I put everything in motion. My first call was to my mom. She was full of questions, but I had no time. As soon as I hung up with her, I called Stacy, who had already planned to come to Dallas with us for the birth (Rennie, too).

My mind was racing as I woke up Aidan. His eyes were groggy as I explained to him what was going on.

"Aidan, it's time. Your brother and sister are coming. We're all driving to Dallas."

Aidan gasped and shot out of bed.

Within ten minutes we had loaded all of our bags into the car. Stacy and Rennie met us in between our front yards. I ran across and hugged Stacy. We both giggled. Our caravan was ready to roll. I called my mom one more time.

"Are y'all ready?"

I already knew the answer to this.

"We'll be about fifteen minutes behind you. Maybe we can meet at a truck stop?"

My adrenaline was up and I didn't want to waste even one second. Even the thought of pulling over to a truck stop and waiting for the Cotton Family Tsunami to roll in made me crazy.

"We'll see y'all in Texas."

This was our first time making the drive to Dallas in the middle of the night. The road was empty, and it was pitch black. I couldn't believe we were finally making the drive to get our babies. This journey had been years in the making. I couldn't stop thinking about how the time had finally come. Dirk was very focused behind the wheel.

"Can you believe it, honey?"

"Yes, I can."

Dirk and I always had this sweet exchange when something momentous was about to happen. It usually started with me asking him if he could believe what was happening, followed by his response of "yes." I know Dirk thought it was silly, but he always played along.

I looked back at Aidan. He was wide awake, looking out the window with his big blue eyes and messy bed hair. He was now riding in the back row of the car with the two car seats in the middle row where he used to sit. These were his final hours as an only child. I was so eager to get to Texas, but I was also trying to soak in these last few minutes as a family of three.

Forty-five minutes later, Brian called to let us know Tiffany was at the hospital being assessed. Her blood pressure was still rising, so a C-section had been scheduled for five in the morning. I breathed a sigh of relief knowing we would arrive in time. As we drove along, I was overwhelmed by my feelings. It reminded me of my wedding day—an indescribable energy that would forever change our lives.

I really thought I had a few more days or weeks. I wondered to myself if I had read enough books on parenting twins. Should I have taken some classes?

"Oh, Lord. Am I prepared to be a mommy of three?" Truthfully, the answer was no, but I had learned this is just how life comes. You can prepare all you want, but the toughest part is being prepared to let go.

It was two in the morning when we finally reached the hotel. Most of the windows were dark. I waited in the car with Aidan while Dirk quickly checked in and grabbed the room keys for my parents. As we pulled out of the parking lot headed for the hospital, I said "Let's go get our babies."

CHAPTER 44

The Calm before the Storm

The day would unfold into a crazy twenty-four hours of multiple births. We had waited for so long, and the time was at long last here.

Sitting in our hospital room, I knew it was the calm before the storm. I welcomed these last moments of peace and tranquility.

Dirk was in the corner of the room quietly charging up his iPhone and his video camera. He was such a total nerd when it came to capturing family events that I affectionately referred to him as Clark Griswold. We never watched the recordings, but we had everything from trips that Dirk and I took before we were married to Aidan's birthday parties and holidays organized and filed away in a desk drawer.

Stacy and Rennie were sitting on the long, narrow bench by the window. Normally Rennie would be cracking jokes, but this morning he was being very quiet. He and Stacy were speaking in hushed tones. I was so happy to have them with us, because they had literally walked this path alongside us.

It was no surprise to find out that my parents were still en route to the hospital, along with my sister and brother-in-law. I had texted with my mom several times. She was wrapping baby gifts on the drive, and they stopped for a quick bite to eat. There was no telling when exactly they would arrive.

One of the labor and delivery nurses came into the room with surgical scrubs, masks, and caps for me and Dirk. She gave us instructions and then surprised us with a small caveat.

"It is totally up to the anesthetist whether or not you are allowed in the delivery room. If it is not safe for Tiffany, you will not be allowed in."

This news made my jaw drop. It was the first time we were hearing about this. Nothing of the sort had been mentioned during the hospital tour. I could tell by Dirk's expression that he was stunned too. I wondered how it was possible that it was left up to one person we had never met to decide whether we could be present for the birth of our children. I tried to decide whether to be calm and logical or scream and cry. I looked over at Dirk and implored him.

"We need to speak to the anesthetist and tell her our story. She needs to know how important this is."

We had already missed the transfer. The thought of missing the birth of our children was unimaginable. I silently prayed that God would whisper in the anesthetist's ear and garner favor so that we could be there.

I decided this was a good time for Dirk and me to check in on Tiffany. We hadn't seen her yet, so we wandered down the hall to her room. She was in her bed hooked up to two fetal monitors, with Brian at her side. Tiffany looked absolutely beautiful. Here face lit up when I walked into the room.

"It's here—can you believe it?" I asked her.

I had a thousand thoughts but didn't want to overwhelm her. I wanted things to be calm for her. I just looked at her with tears in my eyes.

"We're just so grateful. I just want you to know how much we love you. Words cannot begin to express our appreciation for you. You are such an angel!" I gave her a big hug. Tiffany's face broke out into her smile again.

"Aww, we love you guys too," she said.

In that moment, I felt so connected to her. She was more than just our carrier or even a friend. Over the last nine months, our relationship had deepened, and Tiffany had become a sister to me. Dirk and I wanted to pray over her one last time, but for now we knew she needed to rest.

We wandered back to our room, where Aidan was sitting on the hospital bed with his iPad. I couldn't get over how big he looked. I still remembered every last detail about the day he was born. I thought of him as a toddler praying nightly for a sibling, and then as an imaginative six-year-old standing on his bed, raising his voice to the ceiling in case God couldn't hear him.

After all these years, God had finally answered Aidan. He had answered all of our prayers. It wasn't in our time or by our design, but we had stayed faithful, surrendered to His plan, and ultimately God had delivered. It was such a beautiful lesson for all of us, and especially for Aidan.

Every day we consciously tried to teach Aidan about overcoming obstacles by being creative and finding a loophole. This had been a real-life lesson in the power of perseverance, remaining faithful, and trusting that God has a plan. It was a powerful testament, a tool that would serve Aidan for the rest of his life. He crawled into my lap and asked for a back rub. As he leaned into me, I wrapped my arms around him. I wanted to love on my first-born son and let him know the special bond we shared.

"Aidan, I want you to know Mommy loves you so much. No matter what happens after today, no matter how crazy things might get, I want you to know how special you are and how much I love you."

Aidan nodded, gave me a kiss on the cheek, and smiled at me. He had lost another tooth over the weekend, and he looked so cute.

"Do you know why we will always have a special bond?" I asked him.

Aidan shrugged his shoulders.

"Because you are the only baby mommy carried in her tummy."

Aidan's big blue eyes widened. He seemed to understand the profundity of this moment. I gave him a big squeeze. My heart was so full it felt like it might burst, and then *Bam!*—my father busted through the hospital room door with my mother and pregnant sister, who looked like she was ready to pop.

As always, the Cotton Family Tsunami was true to form. My father had his murse (male purse) across his chest and a briefcase in each hand. My mother was carrying a stack of baby gifts and was chewing my dad out for answering the damn phone in the hospital. My sister waddled in behind them with her husband, Andrew, who looked like he had just woken up. Melanie didn't have any makeup on, but she had a beautiful pregnancy glow. As soon as she parted her lips to say hello, she burst into tears.

We had about half an hour before Tiffany's C-section, so we all made our way back to Tiffany's room. The Cotton Family Tsunami swept in behind us, so it wasn't quiet in there for long. Everyone hugged Tiffany and took pictures of her. Melanie took one look at Tiffany's enormous belly and started crying again. My mother peppered Tiffany with endless questions as my father exclaimed at the top of his lungs, "I can't believe this is happening! I just—uh—can't believe it! It's just unbelievable, Tiffany, uh . . ."

The nurse anesthetist walked into the room, so I knew this was our moment. She was already dressed in her scrubs and mask and looked very anonymous. She was very stoic and serious as she addressed us.

"My job is to take care of Tiffany and the babies."

"We completely understand and agree. But if it is at all possible, we would really like to be present for their birth. This has been a very long journey for us. We have lost seven of our babies. It would mean everything to us if we could be in there. I promise we will be quiet and will do exactly what is asked of us," I implored her.

It was a very impersonal conversation. I was a little panicked, but I knew that ultimately it was in God's hands. He knew the desires of our hearts, so we had to trust.

When it was almost time for Tiffany to be wheeled down to the operating room, Brian stood up.

"Alright, people . . ."

He gestured for all of us to gather around Tiffany and hold hands. We bowed our heads and Brian led us in a prayer.

"God, thank you for this entire journey. Everything that the O'Haras have gone through has pointed to and is a beautiful picture of Your faithfulness on this day. God, you didn't forget their dreams. Today you have given all of us a manifestation of Your faithfulness. I pray for the entire team of doctors and nurses that will be in the room with Tiffany. Guide them, Lord. Thank you, God, for completing the work perfectly on this day. We pray for Tiffany and the babies and ask that you protect them during the birthing process and ask that everything goes perfectly."

Between crying spells, my sister managed to pray over us. She asked God to bless us and thanked Tiffany for her amazing and selfless act. There were already a lot of wet eyes in the room when Rennie joined in the prayer.

"Lord, we are all so excited for this moment with our best friends. I remember the countless prayers, numerous tears, and more prayers. This is the anticipation of a promise fulfilled. The path was not as any of us originally planned, but You have come through on Your promise. I also remember the steadfastness of their pain and disappointment. It would have been so easy for Dirk and Steph to stop, to give up on Your promise. But God, you were true and Dirk and Steph were faithful—and now we are about to have their beautiful twins."

I could feel the excitement in the room. A nurse popped in and looked at Tiffany.

"Okay, Tiffany, are you ready?"

Tiffany's eyes lit up she calmly responded.

"Yes," she said, and smiled.

We all filed out of the room so Tiffany and Brian could have a moment together. My heart started racing as we walked back down the long hall. A flood of memories came rushing into my head; all of the positive pregnancy tests, sitting on Angela's couch in tears for hours, and waking up after my painful D&Cs in the recovery room. I thought about miscarrying in church and Dirk holding me when my heart felt like it was breaking. I felt a small smile spreading across my face when I thought about the day the girls surprised me in Dirk's convertible wearing their sheik headwear, trying to cheer me up.

My thoughts were interrupted by the nurse who came in to tell us that Tiffany was being prepped for surgery. I breathed a huge sigh of relief when the nurse told us the anesthetist had given permission for us to be in the room for the birth. I looked up at the ceiling and mouthed, "thank you."

Dirk and I could barely contain our excitement as we pulled on our white scrubs, booties, and caps. Since neither one of us is a big person, we looked completely ridiculous in the oversized surgical scrubs. We laughed when we realized that in every picture we took with our newborn twins, we would both be memorialized as the Stay Puft Marshmallow Man from *Ghostbusters*.

CHAPTER 45

"Out of the Everywhere Into the Here"

In the ten years that Dirk and I had been married, he had never liked my use of the word *surreal* to describe moments that were unreal or strange. Anytime I said it, it was guaranteed my husband would furrow his thick O'Hara eyebrows. As we walked into the operating room, the surrealistic moment washed over me: we were about to watch someone else give birth to our biological children. But today I had a better word, and it was *divine*.

God was present in the room. His energy was indescribable, but it was all around us. We were surrounded by spheres of light, and the colors in the room gleamed bright white and heavenly blue. I could feel angels watching over us, protecting us and the three medical teams in the room. The sound of all three heartbeats—Tiffany's and the twins'—coming from the monitor made me so emotional I was worried I might pass out.

The anesthetist immediately barked orders at us. She pointed to two chairs in the corner of the room and told us to remain seated until both babies were born and in their bassinets. We were so grateful to be in there, we wanted to follow the letter of the law. Dirk of course wanted to record the birth. It felt like we were before a judge as he asked permission from the commanding anesthetist, and I could see the relief on Dirk's face when she said yes. As soon as Dirk and I took our seats and Dr. Roberts signaled he was good to go, the anesthetist walked over to Tiffany and completely changed her demeanor.

"Thank you, Tiffany. You are doing the most amazing thing for this family."

I wasn't sure what had softened her heart, but I was happy to see it. The room grew quiet as the surgical teams worked in focused unison. All of a sudden, I heard the voice of one of the nurses.

"Five forty-three!"

This was followed by the sound of a baby crying. There, not ten feet in front of us, was our precious baby girl. It was a shock to see her—she was tiny and so beautiful. She had a little bit of dark hair on her head. I was overwhelmed by emotion as I watched the nurse wipe her off with a towel and place her in a bassinet. I had to resist the urge to stand. Instead, I spoke to her from where I was seated.

"Hi sweet girl, we love you! Welcome to the world! Happy Birthday!"

A moment later, the voice of a second nurse boomed.

"Five forty-four!"

I heard Dirk giggle, and then there was a different cry. It was the sound of our baby boy wailing. I was flooded with so much emotion that I was short of breath.

"Oh, my goodness! Oh—my gosh. Is this really real? Oh, my Lord. Thank you, Jesus."

I ran over to our little boy's bassinet. I just marveled at him. He didn't have as much hair as his sister, but what he had was platinum blond— just like Aidan's had been.

"Hi sweet boy! Oh my gosh, Happy Birthday!"

They were both so beautiful, I couldn't take my eyes off of either one of them. They were truly two living miracles. I laughed at myself because I couldn't figure out which one of them to go to.

Our baby girl gave another short cry and then stopped abruptly. That's when I noticed she was turning blue. The nurse who was holding her spoke out.

"She's having some trouble breathing."

I panicked as I watched my little girl struggle to take a breath. It was absolutely terrifying. "No, no way," I thought. I immediately started praying over her. It was the longest minute of our lives watching one of the doctors calmly give her oxygen. She wasn't breathing and turned purple.

"Did you over-stim her?" the anesthetist asked her nurse.

"I think I might have."

The anesthetist calmly gave our baby girl a second puff of oxygen. A full minute had gone by at this point.

Finally, our tiny daughter took a deep breath and cried. The crisis was over. I was so relieved. In the meantime, our poor little son screamed at the top of his lungs as a nurse took his rectal temperature.

I couldn't help but cry with emotion as Dirk and I took the babies over to Tiffany. I had known from the moment we met Tiffany that on the day of their birth, I wanted her to see them immediately. She had taken care of them on the first part of their journey, and as the torch was handed over to us, we wanted her to see who she had been carrying all of this time. She was a little out of it from the anesthesia, but still present enough that she cried as she admired the two miracles that had been inside of her for the last nine months.

It was unbelievable. I had given birth to one of our children, and watched someone else give birth to our other two children. Not many women have had such a viewpoint.

After the nurse took their weight and footprints, I just stared and stared at them. I sat down in a chair and Dirk handed me our little girl, while the nurse handed me our little boy. Here I was—holding our babies. They were nuzzled into my neck. I drank them in. I loved how they smelled and I loved their little whimpers. I felt like I was at home. There was no better feeling in the world. God was literally wrapping me in love. I kissed them what seemed like a thousand times. The feeling was indescribable. Our prayers had been answered. Not on our terms, not on our time. But they had been answered.

"Thank you," I said as I looked up. Tears rolled down my cheeks.

After a few minutes, the babies were wrapped in blankets and placed in a clear plastic bassinet facing one another. This was the first time in nine months they had come face-to-face with one another. I gushed when our baby girl put her little hand up to her face as she lay next to her little brother. And now it was time for both of them to meet their big brother.

Today was the day that Aidan had finally gotten to wear his specially designed "Only Child" T-shirt with the words crossed out and "Big Brother" written beneath them. He gasped and smiled the biggest smile when he met his baby brother and baby sister, whom he had prayed for through so many years.

We had already planned for Aidan to be the one to introduce the babies and announce their names to our loved ones, who were all anxiously waiting to meet them. Unlike when we announced Aidan's name as Presley Hereford, this time around Dirk didn't have any pranks planned.

It was Christmas all over again for Aidan as he stared down at his brother and sister.

"Will you whisper their names to me?"

Although Aidan had loved Russell and KayDee, we had opted for a couple of other names that would be more meaningful to our family. It fell on me to deliver the news.

"Listen, we didn't pick the names you wanted. So, I will tell you the girl's name and Daddy will tell you the boy's name. Okay?"

Aidan nodded eagerly.

"Okay! Be quiet, be quiet," he said. "Don't let anyone hear you."

I continued, "Your sister's name is Stella Jane."

He gasped with excitement, and then Dirk leaned in.

"And your brother's name is Smith Patrick."

The newly appointed big brother of two looked down adoringly at his siblings.

"Hello Smith. Hello Stella."

I cried.

After practicing his announcement a couple of times, Aidan was completely comfortable and ready to introduce his baby brother and sister to their family for the first time. He had worn what I called his "full pull" athletic socks and his rainbow Kevin Durant sneakers for the occasion.

Dirk and I walked on either side of Aidan as he wheeled the babies down the hallway to our room. When we were just outside, I slipped in first with my iPhone so I could capture Aidan's announcement from the perspective of my family. All eyes were on Aidan as he proudly pushed the bassinet into the room. Dirk was right behind him with his video camera ready to go. Everybody gasped as they laid eyes on the babies for the very first time. My sister jumped up and fumbled with her iPhone.

"Wait! Wait!"

Then my father stood up with his iPhone as well.

"Well, hold on. I'm not ready either. Hold on."

When my mother stood up and completely blocked Dirk's view of Aidan and the babies, I realized I should have walked my family through a rehearsal. Aidan smiled as he pointed at his little brother.

"So, this one is Smith Patrick O'Hara."

Right then I saw my mom's jaw drop.

"Wait a minute, what now?"

It felt so good to see how touched she was that her family name would live on through her newborn grandson. Aidan moved his little hand toward his sister.

"And this is Stella Jane O'Hara."

My sister's voice trembled with emotion as she looked at the babies.

"So, we've got Stella and Smith. Alright, Stella and Smith. They're just so cute!"

My mom kept repeating their names over and again.

"Now, which one is the boy?" my dad asked.

We all laughed as Aidan pointed to Smith's blue cap. Then we gushed when Stella yawned.

When the pomp and circumstance was over, we let Aidan hold his siblings. Then we took them in to see Tiffany and Brian. Tiffany teared up as she took Stella in her arms and gazed over at Smith in Brian's arms. I kissed her on the forehead.

"You are our angel."

She smiled at me and at the babies. We knew we would forever be connected by these two little miracles and the path we had walked together.

We had bought gifts for Tiffany, Brian, and their daughters. Tiffany smiled her thanks sweetly.

"We bought a gift for Aidan. It's an electronic fart machine," Brian said proudly.

Tiffany rolled her eyes.

"Clearly, I wasn't present when they bought it," she said.

We both laughed. We were definitely all part of the same family now.

All throughout the previous night, we had been in touch with Dirk's parents. They were very happy and emotional. We had texted them pictures and given them hourly updates. They planned to make the drive out in the afternoon to meet their new grandchildren.

In the meantime, Dirk and I settled in to feed the babies and have some skin-on-skin bonding time. Stella was so soulful, and Smith, I could already tell, had the personality of a showman.

Even as I held them in my arms, I couldn't believe they were really here. I thought about everything that had happened over the last six years. My seven babies in heaven. God had restored what was lost. He had healed my broken heart. In just a few hours, my sister would give birth to her own daughter. I took this as a sign from God that He was present. He did not restore my body to what I had wanted, but He had made me steadfast and strong.

God had given me beauty for ashes; oil of joy instead of mourning; a garment of praise instead of the spirit of despair. As for the Cotton Family Tsunami, they rolled out of Texas as only they could, having doubled their number of grandchildren in just one long Labor Day weekend.

When we finally got the babies home and into their cribs, I couldn't take my eyes off of them. Neither could Dirk. I could have stood there all day and night. As we watched them sleep, I couldn't help but start up the sweet little game we always played.

"Can you believe they're here, honey?"

I already knew his answer, but I waited with bated breath. Dirk smiled.

"Yes, I can."

As we watched the babies sleep, I thought of "Baby," one of my favorite poems, written by George Macdonald:

WHERE did you come from, baby dear?
Out of the everywhere into the here.

Where did you get those eyes so blue?
Out of the sky as I came through.

What makes the light in them sparkle and spin?
Some of the starry spikes left in.

Where did you get that little tear?
I found it waiting when I got here.

What makes your forehead so smooth and high?
A soft hand strok'd it as I went by.

What makes your cheek like a warm white rose?
I saw something better than any one knows.

Whence that three-corner'd smile of bliss?
Three angels gave me at once a kiss.

Where did you get this pearly ear?
God spoke, and it came out to hear.

Where did you get those arms and hands?
Love made itself into bonds and bands.

Feet, whence did you come, you darling things?
From the same box as the cherubs' wings.

How did they all just come to be you?
God thought about me, and so I grew.

But how did you come to us, you dear?
God thought about you, and so I am here.

EPILOGUE

On the first night we brought Stella and Smith home, I stayed in the nursery for hours just staring at them. I just couldn't believe they were here. I knew rest would be at a premium but even as they slept soundly, I wouldn't let myself slip away to the master bedroom. They were two living miracles and I could not take my eyes off of them. They are almost five years old now and not a day goes by that I don't marvel at our journey.

We have had momentous days, like the one about two months after they were born when I hung the "S" gate ornament from Gigi's house on the wall in the nursery. It was a big day and I was so happy to pay tribute to my family and bring a little part of Gigi into the nursery. She would have been crazy about these babies.

We've also had many a poop explosion, and as Stella and Smith have grown, so have their twin shenanigans. Dirk and I have actually slept a lot less than we thought we would and on more than one occasion, I have fallen asleep at the end of the day fully clothed, shoes and all on my bed. Life with twins probably would have been easier had I been seven years younger. Still, I would not change a thing. There were lessons to be learned along the way, and the mountains I climbed to finally reach my babies brought me closer to God and deepened my faith.

I know it is hard for people to understand that I never blamed God for my miscarriages. I was frustrated and there were many days when I demanded to know why this was happening, but I never felt abandoned by Him. The fingerprints of His love were always around me. He showed up by sending me angels—Pastor Linda when I needed her most, Giuliana Rancic when I prayed for a sign, and of course, our surrogate, Tiffany.

I believed then, as I do now, that God knew the desires of my heart and that He wanted to deliver them to me. He did ask me to dig deep and to climb mountains. At other times He asked for patience and stillness (which by the way does not come naturally to me). As I scaled those rocky paths not always knowing what lay ahead for me, it took grit to continue trudging onward. With every twist and turn where I progressed forward, I also learned *to trust* in His timing and in His plan.

I realize that this is a very progressive view of God. Even I chuckle a bit that I am a modern girl living in the Bible Belt who doesn't believe enjoying a glass of wine with girlfriends and being faithful are mutually exclusive. Very simply, I believe that God is love.

During my six-year infertility journey, God challenged me to fulfill my potential and become the woman I had always envisioned being. He did this so I could be the kind of wife and mother I am today.

One day He also laid it on my heart to write this book. I've always believed that with great privilege comes great responsibility. So, on the day that God encouraged my heart to deliver his message of love and hope, I took His calling seriously. This book was a four-year project. I wrote it not just for women suffering from infertility, but for anyone who is suffering, lost, isolated, or just searching.

I believe the world today is ready for this message. I pray that it brings you comfort and peace, and encourages you to spread your wings and fly!

ACKNOWLEDGMENTS

To God—thank You for Your amazing power and work in our lives, for Your goodness and countless blessings. For without them, the achievement of this book would not have been possible. I am truly blessed and remain your humble servant.

To my amazing husband, Dirk, my knight in shining armor—this book would not have been written if it weren't for your love, wisdom, patience, support, and encouragement. Thank you for wiping every tear and for keeping me strong. I am so lucky to wake up next to you every morning, and love the beautiful family that we have made together.

To my beloved children: Aidan, my first-born son, the one who made me a mother—I am so proud of you. You taught me to *never* give up, and to be *bold* in prayer. Always stay humble and kind. To my miracle twins—Stella, my precious and beautiful daughter, my "best girl"; Smith, my youngest son, who is so full of joy. Trust in the Lord; you will never be disappointed. Daddy and I dreamed about you for so long and believed that you would be ours. I hope that one day when you are grown, you will dust this book off and after reading it, be reaffirmed in how much you are loved and how much you were wanted.

To our angel, our surrogate Tiffany Baker, and her family, Brian, Trinity, and Selah—it is hard to find words to thank someone for carrying your children. Dirk and I are forever indebted to all of you! Thank you for blessing us with the gift of life—twice over! We pray that Stella and Smith will be filled with the same strength and selflessness that you had during their pregnancy, Tiffany. You will have many jewels in your Heavenly crown for all of your earthly good deeds.

I would like to express my sincere love to my parents—to my

mother, Joan Cotton, thank you for giving me a soft place to fall, for helping me after every procedure and loss, and for being a wonderful mom and nana. I love you and couldn't have done this without you! To my father, Chuck Cotton; your encouragement and belief in miracles during our infertility journey was fundamental. Thank you for instilling such determination and tenacity in me.

I would like to thank my little sister, Melanie Obriotti, and her husband, Andrew—you see me at my best and my worst and love me anyway. Thank you for all of the support over the journey. Sister to sister we will always be, a couple of nuts off the family tree.

To my in-laws, Forrest and Loretta O'Hara—I won the lottery when it comes to the two of you. You have shown me unconditional love . . . and you have raised your son to be the man of my dreams. I am so proud and honored to be an O'Hara!

To Stacy Cook, my bestie, and her husband, Rennie—we have laughed and cried together over the last 16 years. Anything is possible when you have the right people there to support you. Your friendship is truly one of my biggest blessings.

To my grandmother in Heaven, Gigi—thank you for showing me to pray for miracles, and for being my angel up above. Your name will live on through Stella and Kate.

To our family—the Spains, the Obriottis, the Bairds, the O'Haras, the Kesslers; and to our extended families: the Sipes, O'Haras, Phillipses, and Smiths. Thank you for giving us warmth and love, and for being such caring and fun aunts, uncles, and cousins to our children.

To Melissa and Ben Houston—thank you for your unwavering friendship, your many prayers and candle lightings, and for always bringing the party hat. BDKK.

To my Angel Wings team: My editor, Brenda Aréchiga—you are more than a spotlight. You are a bright star who shines for the benefit of others. Thank you for going on this journey with me, and helping me to find the perfect words for my story. To my wickedly talented web designer, Tone Stray, thank you for bringing my vision to life! I would also like to thank Sharon Honeycutt, my amazing proofreader, and Megan Fonk, my intern.

To my bridesmaids and longtime friends Sherry Snell-Jones, Valerie Schulz, Stacey Darnell, Linda Szuhy, and Masha Trainor. Life is about great friends and amazing adventures. There is nothing I wouldn't do for each of you!

Thanks to everyone at Plum Bay Publishing. I am grateful to Claire McKinney, my insightful publisher; to Keely Flanagan, my social media expert; to Barbara Aronica, the greatest cover designer I could ever imagine; and to Kate Petrella, my ever-patient copy editor.

To God's favorite little Sunday school class—thank you for going on the ride with us. Dirk and I cherish your prayers and friendships.

I would like to thank those who have been like family to us—Dirk's business team and the Tuttle FUMC Women.

I want to express my deepest gratitude to all of the health practitioners involved in our journey: Dr. Schoolcraft and staff, Dr. Craig, Dr. Hansen, Dr. Allison and staff, Dr. Kuhls and staff, and Dr. John Paul Roberts and staff. God bless you all!

I wish to recognize the valuable help and support of my angels: Kim Jackson, my Pilates instructor; Susan, who gave me the gift of prayer; Pastor Linda and the McFarlin church staff, who showed us compassion and love in the face of grief; my life coach, Jacqueline Cornaby, for elevating me; my counselor, Angela, for your wisdom; and to Amy Pomerantz and Olivia Colts-Tegg—thank you for loving our children as your own.

To my Norman friends—Kathleen Shuler, Apryl Meyer, Emily Leidner, Libbi Holbrook, Julie Sparks, Melanie Moulton, and Valerie White. Your sweet friendships refresh my soul. Thank you for believing in our miracle babies, even when they were just a dream!

I wholeheartedly express my sincere thanks to two of my angels: Giuliana Rancic, my burning bush; and Kate Stanton, for making an introduction that forever changed lives.

We want to pay our regards to those who helped us navigate through our surrogacy journey—Shiva Landry from Shared Conception; our lawyers, Virginia Frank and Jenny Womack; and everyone at Texas Health Presbyterian Hospital.

To the women of Junior League of Norman—I have made so many meaningful connections and friendships here that are forever woven in my heart and in this journey.

A special thank-you to my bandmates, Trace, Neil, Lance, Alex, Scott, Dave—being on stage with you was the best therapy (and still is). I am grateful for each of you!

To the entire Norman community—thank you for loving and embracing us and our story.

To anyone I have forgotten . . . please forgive me. Twin mom brain.

Printed in Great Britain
by Amazon